"It takes courage not to walk out on your story, to keep the conversation going with Abba in the beautiful mess of undoneness and brokenness. Chad invites us into just such a story. It's a sacred invitation into his journey for more, no matter the cost!"

Rich Hodge, investor in people/missionary,
YWAM South Africa

"This book offers a fresh perspective on living naturally supernatural. In a time where our world seems to be fascinated with all things paranormal, this book could not have come at a better time. I found that Chad's humor, personal experience and revelation on the kindness of Father not only encouraged me but propelled me toward a life of 'signs, wonders and miracles.' This is not for superstars, or specially gifted ministers, but all those who follow Jesus and His Dad. Simply put, this is one man's story of how Jesus opened his eyes to a different reality. My prayer is that this becomes yours."

Rich Butler, lead pastor, City Church, Simpsonville and
Greenville, South Carolina, wearecitychurch.com

# SIGNS,
## WONDERS
### *and a*
## BAPTIST PREACHER

# SIGNS, WONDERS

### and a

## BAPTIST PREACHER

How JESUS FLIPPED MY WORLD UPSIDE DOWN

## CHAD NORRIS

**Chosen**
a division of Baker Publishing Group
Minneapolis, Minnesota

Published by Chosen Books
11400 Hampshire Avenue South
Bloomington, Minnesota 55438
www.chosenbooks.com

Chosen Books is a division of
Baker Publishing Group, Grand Rapids, Michigan

Printed in the United States of America

Library of Congress Cataloging-in-Publication Data
Norris, Chad.
    Signs, wonders, and a Baptist preacher : how Jesus flipped my world upside down / Chad Norris.
        p.   cm.
    Summary: "A humorous, honest account of how the world of a staunch Southern Baptist preacher turned upside down when he encountered the Person of the Holy Spirit"—Provided by publisher.
    ISBN 978-0-8007-9540-5 (pbk. : alk. paper)
    1. Norris, Chad. 2. Baptists—United States—Clergy—Biography.
I. Title.
BX6495.N58A3 2013
286.092—dc23
[B]                                                           2012040230

Cover design by Gearbox

13   14   15   16   17   18   19        7   6   5   4   3   2   1

## To Wendy

I remember when we were dating and we agreed that the path He had for us would not be normal. It will be fun to continue to see what He does with us. From that day in the counselor's office when Jesus flipped me upside down until now, you have never questioned whether or not this pursuit is real. The greatest blessing He has given me is you. Thank you for being a rock when I did not know which way was up. You bring joy to our family. Our three little people think you are the most incredible woman in the world. I do, too.

# Contents

# Foreword

Chad's grades from the University of Georgia made it impossible for him to study theology in a seminary. He wasn't unhappy about this because he never wanted to attend seminary. All he wanted to do was lead young people to Christ. And he was already successfully preaching Christ to crowds of young people around the country. So it made no sense to Chad when he heard God tell him to apply for seminary. It made perfect sense to Chad when he received a letter of rejection from the seminary two weeks after he had applied.

Then God pulled one of those impossible strings, and Chad was in seminary with his new wife, Miss University of Georgia. Along with Wendy, Chad also took his bottles of Klonopin and Zoloft to seminary as well. The supernatural peace that transcends human understanding, which we Christians claim as our unique possession, had eluded Chad since he was five. He lived in a nightmare world of panic attacks and depression. The young man who preached peace to the young had so little of it himself.

Chad did not distinguish himself academically at the seminary, nor did the seminary heal Chad of the panic attacks and depression. But some special professors took a special interest in him, and that is probably why God sent him to seminary.

After Chad graduated, he went right back to telling young people about Christ. He never thought in a million years that he would write a book. Then God healed him of the panic and depression. Then God used him to heal others. Then Chad had a new story to tell.

Then God pulled another one of those impossible strings. And you are now holding Chad's first book in your hands. I say "first book" because I think the One writing Chad's story has a few more impossible twists and turns for the young man.

Chad is still learning how to tell his story, but he is a quick learner. He speaks in the vernacular that endears him to young audiences. He is a little too repetitive for my literary tastes, but he is not teaching creative writing. He is teaching about the creative power of God. Another defect of the book is that Chad can't completely conceal his anger over the bruising he has received at the hands of Christians who don't believe that God heals as much or as often as Chad claims. I know about that anger. I am not too worried about it because I know the power that heals it.

Lastly, this is not a theological book. It is a story. Chad knows that a theologian would slaughter him in a debate. But he's not debating. He is simply telling his story. It is a story of redemption and grace and healing and love. It is the story of a young man experiencing the Jesus of the New Testament. And a young man with an experience of Jesus will never be at the mercy of a theologian with an argument.

A man who could not read once won a debate with a group of erudite theologians when he told them, "One thing I do know. Once I was blind, but now I see."

I love theologians. I used to be one. Still, I would rather have Chad pray for me than any doctor of theology that I know.

Jack Deere, teaching pastor, Wellspring Church,
Dallas/Fort Worth, Texas; bestselling author,
*Surprised by the Power of the Spirit*

# *Acknowledgments*

Writing this book has been interesting to say the least. As I have fleshed out the story of my life, I have even found myself thinking, *I'm still processing how odd life can be when God does something out of my normal way of looking at things.* I simply want to say that the thoughts that I share in this work are my own. Everything that I have written is from my own experience in following Jesus. These thoughts in no way reflect the ideas or theology of the organizations that I have worked with or people I have done life with. I gave my life to Jesus Christ when I was twelve years old, and this book is an honest reflection of what He has shown me in my pursuit of Him.

I want to thank Jesus for helping me at my worst moment. I love You. My life is Yours.

Thank you to Wendy. You are the strongest person I know.

Thank you to Sam, Ruthie and Jack. You three are not just my children—you are my friends.

Thank you to Rich Butler. You are an incredible leader. Thank you for letting me be "me." Your authentic passion for Jesus Christ is refreshing. I have never been around a leader hungrier for His presence than you. I cannot wait to see what the Father continues to do with City Church.

Thank you to Ben Daniel. I will never forget the early stages of conversations about the Kingdom. I hope we never lose our childlike wonder. You show us all what it means to invest in others. Your influence in my life is priceless.

Thank you to the entire City Church Staff for listening to me ramble on and on about the manuscript. City Church is my extended family. Coming to work is fun. Working with family is a gift. What we have is special.

To City Church. I am grateful to Abba that I get to be a part of this church family. I have always been drawn to real people. When I think about City Church, I think about the words *authentic* and *hungry*. I pray we stay hungry until He returns.

Thank you to Dave Rhodes. Beeson and Wayfarer stretched me beyond what I thought I was capable of. We took a chance at an idea and had fun doing it. 3DM is lucky to have you. Change the world.

To the entire Wayfarer team: I love you. I meet people on a monthly basis in Greenville who talk about the impact of Engage. We grew, we learned, and we laughed.

Thank you to Robert Neely for walking beside me and helping this book come to life. Without you, I would have never been able to write this. You are great at what you do, and you are a true brother. Your integrity and humility is something I rarely see. You make me want to love Jesus more.

Thank you to Mark and Amanda Combs. Without you this book would never have gotten off the ground. Who knew that a healed shoulder would lead to this? You two are contagiously authentic. Wendy and I love your family.

To Chad Johnson. In every season I have gone through the last twenty years, you have been there to help shape my "story." You have never judged me. You listen better than anyone I know. Your impact on my life comes through these pages. I have always felt safe with you as I flesh out all of these different Kingdom thoughts. You, Angie and the boys are family.

I would like to thank everyone who took the time to read so many rough drafts of this work. I truly am grateful for your work and your friendship.

Thank you, Mom and Dad. I can still remember sitting around our table in Shoresbrook when I asked so many questions about what I wrote about in this book. I will never be able to repay you two for the investment you made in me. I love you both.

Gabe Norris, I love you more than I can express. Calvin told us at Beeson that the true definition of a leader is this: "Simply turn around. If no one is following you, you are not a leader. If people are standing in line to follow, then you know you are a leader." I have never seen someone who has more people willing to follow him than you. Thank you for helping me think through this book. Thank you for listening. Thank you for believing in me. I cannot imagine two brothers on the earth closer than we are.

Bumpsie, you are the best sister I could ever have asked for. I wrote so much about Mama Jane in this book, and I can see her legacy coming through you. Thank you for your fierce loyalty to our family. I love you.

Thank you, Justin, for convincing me that I could write this book. Thank you for believing in me. I love you.

To our Men's Group. Who knew that a bunch of holy misfits engaging in real conversations on the Kingdom would lead me to this? I love all of you. I am a better person as a result of our times together.

Thank you to Rich Hodge. Dustin said it best: "You are Peter Pan and we are the lost boys." I have had some neat people pour into my life, but none of them can match what Jesus has done with me through your influence. No way I would have ever written this book without knowing you.

Thank you to Gary Hypolitte. Your hunger for God is intoxicating. I love you deeply. When all of this is over, I will sit back and relish the fact that I got to know you. Your walk with Jesus is inspiring. My time with you in Haiti has changed my life.

Thank you, Mama Jane and Papa. I miss you both. I will see you both soon.

Thank you to Jack Deere. When I was in seminary, you were a hero to me. You are a pioneer. Thank you for opening my eyes to a bigger view of God. It is humbling that you are writing the foreword to my book. Thank you for your honest critique.

Lastly, thank You, Father. When You opened my eyes to how kind You are, I could not believe it. I love You. My life is Yours.

# *Introduction*

Another Haiti trip was in the books. Our plane lifted off the ground at Port Au Prince for the return flight home, and I could already taste the cheeseburger I would order as soon as we landed in Miami. I had two things on my mind: Taking a hot shower, and savoring that cheeseburger. I looked around the plane and saw that many of our team members were journaling about their time in Haiti. I decided I was too tired so I leaned my head back in order to sleep, and that is when I knew things were about to change.

*I want you to write a book, Chad,* is all I heard. I heard it in that place where you cannot talk yourself out of it. I said softly to God, "I don't want to write a book because I know what You want me to write about. I don't want to end up on one of those web pages that will call me a crazy person and a heretic." I quickly put on headphones and started listening to music.

Two weeks later, I was sitting on a couch in our church office and I said, "Fine, I'll do it, Lord."

Before we even get started with this book, there are a few things I want to get out of the way: I do not think I have

God all figured out; I would get slaughtered in a biblical debate with scholars; I do not seek sensational things about the Kingdom; I am a laid-back guy who tends to drive very slowly in my minivan with 289,000 miles on it; I am more comfortable around real people with real problems than I am in religious circles; and the biggest desire of my life is to build great friendship with God.

I never thought in a million years I would write a book like this. After all, let's be honest—signs and wonders are strange and even weird. And I never wanted to be known as weird. But in my journey of getting to know God better, some weird things started happening—for example, praying for someone and watching him or her be dramatically healed right in front of my eyes. That is bizarre. It may not be bizarre for you, but for me it has been.

Not long ago, I was sitting beside a swimming pool in Daniel Island, South Carolina, in a casual conversation with one of my best friends. The last thing on my mind was praying for someone's hurting shoulder. To be honest, it was nice to unplug and just soak up some rays while we contemplated the upcoming football season. Another man walked past us and my friend said, "That guy right there is named Mark. He played college football at Wofford, and he knows a good friend of yours."

I walked up to Mark, introduced myself and told him that I grew up minutes away from Wofford College. We swapped stories, and I asked him casually, "Is your shoulder bothering you?"

He looked at me for a few seconds and smiled. "Chad, I'm in physical therapy for my shoulder right now. How did you know my shoulder is hurting?"

I said, "I've been asking myself that question a lot. The quick answer is 'God showed me.' The long answer is 'I don't know how all of this really works.' I just know that I have to pray for you." Then in the midst of a lot of people swimming and relaxing in the sun, I prayed for my new friend and God healed him. Nobody knew we were praying. I did not call attention to the situation. I prayed a quick prayer and Mark said, "It feels better." He never went back to physical therapy, and we have been engaged in conversations about the Kingdom ever since.

As a result of this random encounter, Mark ended up leading a Men's Hike at the church I serve. From that hike, many men's lives have been changed for the better. That night I lay in bed and told God, "Thank You for reminding me of how real You are."

In this book, I hope to help you experience this bizarre God just as I have. It all started for me when I really read the Bible. Have you ever been transported? I have not. Acts talks about this. I have never seen anyone raised from the dead either (not yet, that is).

Once I started reading the Bible and following what I found there, I began to go deeper and deeper into the Kingdom of God. So for me, the days of proclamation without demonstration are over. I have seen too much. I have heard too much.

When you are wrecked by Jesus' wild passion and love for you and the way in which He wants His Kingdom presented, you tend to care more about what He thinks than what other people think. At least that has been the case for me. Now, please refrain from picturing me as a vigilante. This book is not my attempt to stir the pots of religious thought or to put myself on an island. (That may happen, but it is not my goal.)

Instead, I am just agreeing with Peter and John. They said in Acts 4:20 that they could not stop talking about what they had seen and heard. The same is true for me.

Recently in our church, at a service called Hosting His Presence, I prayed for a young man whom I did not know. I said, "Hey, my name is Chad."

The young man said, "My name is Ben. Do you mind listening to the Lord and praying over me?"

Just as we train our people to do, I internally asked the Holy Spirit to calm my mind, and I listened for God to speak to me. I then began to tell Ben what I was hearing. I said, "Ben, you don't need to be skeptical of things like this. The Lord really loves you. I actually see your life taking a dramatic turn very soon. God has something up His sleeve for you. You are incredibly gifted and are called by Him. Brace yourself for change."

Ben replied, "Actually, I am going for a while to Redding, California, to Bethel Church for a visit."

I shook my head. "You won't be moving back here. This trip is a setup for you. God has something planned for you there."

I learned later that Ben did move to Redding and was asked to join the team at Jesus Culture. He now serves on their creative team.

A young man standing beside Ben that night was named Seth. I turned to Seth and said, "I see you sitting on a deck in London reading C. S. Lewis."

Seth smiled and said, "Bro, I just returned from London, and I am getting ready to head back there. I love reading C. S. Lewis." What did God show all three of us that night?

Well, that He is closer than we think, that He is more real than we think, and that what was available for superstars like Peter, James and John is also a reality for normal people like me and you.

Now, when I say this, many people have a quick response: "Be careful, buddy. Don't go down some irresponsible rabbit trail here." Some people cannot even let me finish telling a story about a healing before they jump in and protest it passionately. I get that. I really do. That is why I am going to tell you my whole story—not just the signs and wonders part.

My own story is one of depression and panic attacks. I have been to the darkest corner of the dark night of the soul. I do not have all of the answers, and I have had enough disappointment with God to last me a long time. You will read about that in this book. But through it all, what I have seen and heard has made me wonder why in the world we do not at least see some of the same powerful, miraculous, unexplainable things that our Master saw.

Now some of these same folks who protest the evidence of miracles taking place today get quite passionate about the importance of feeding the poor. They welcome the idea of being completely sold out to Jesus if it involves finances or caring for widows and orphans. Of course, those things find their roots in the biblical text.

But I feel as though we need to notice some other things in the Gospel message as well. I suspect that the Father, Jesus and the Holy Spirit are waiting to see if anyone on earth wants to do what Peter, Stephen, Paul and Philip did. I remember years ago when it dawned on me, "Wait a minute, these people were just normal people. I'm a person just like them." That perhaps is the most elementary thought I have ever had, yet it really got me yearning to dig a little deeper.

And let's move past labels. I doubt, for instance, that Paul went around saying he was *charismatic*. Maybe what I have been calling "extreme" the New Testament calls "ordinary." Take the story of Eutychus. Eutychus fell asleep during Paul's sermon, fell headlong out of a window and died. Paul must have been an incredibly boring preacher, or else so ridiculously long-winded that he preached until it was very late. Nevertheless, Paul did not launch into a sermon about the glory God was getting from this tragedy. He walked downstairs, raised Eutychus from the dead and went back to preaching. That is truly strange. I would have a hard time believing it myself if it were not in that beautiful book called Acts.

I have been a Baptist all of my life, and I am noticing something interesting happening in America. The supernatural has moved away from charismatic-only conversations. In my city, a few traditional Methodist and Presbyterian churches have healing services once a week. Stories of the impossible are starting to rise from unlikely places. By the time my children are raising their own children, I have a sneaking suspicion that the Church will look a lot more like it did when the King was here doing the works of His Father.

So my point in this book is this: I simply want to explore whether or not it is possible to operate on this planet in the way that Jesus commanded His disciples to operate. It is time to put our old paradigms down for a while. Actions we consider abnormal are really quite normal to the One who spoke the world out of nothing. I want my normal to match Jesus' normal.

Jesus has stretched me more than anyone I have ever known. You would think that the closer you get to someone the simpler things would become. That has not been my experience. As a matter of fact, He leaves me scratching my head a lot. His invitation to follow Him brings with it a very high level of challenge.

I am not sure where this story ends. At this point in my life, I do not really care. God told Abram to pick up his family and head out. Abram did not know where he was going, but he knew that he could not stay where he was. All people of faith can relate to that. I know I can. I used to be obsessed with where this journey will take me, but not anymore. I used to be paranoid about what others think of the things that the Father is doing through me. Not anymore. Life is too short to worry about things like that.

So with that said, here is my story. This is the best way I can tell you what I have seen and heard. I sincerely pray that you will find hope for your own situation as you take a look at my own. For me, I count it as a win if you simply choose to wrestle with John 14:12 as a result of reading this book:

[Jesus said,] "Very truly I tell you, whoever believes in me will do the works I have been doing, and they will do even greater things than these, because I am going to the Father."

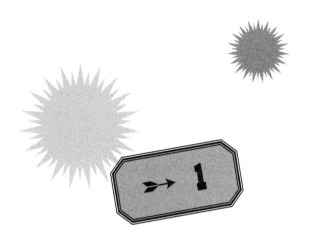

# An Unexpected
# Journey

I like sweet tea, and I like a lot of it. Someone asked me the other day, "What are some of the things you like?" I said that I like good weather, good friends, college football and having a fan on while I sleep. It does not take a lot to make me happy. I am a front-porch-on-the-swing type of guy.

I also like simple things. I like to say that *simple* is the new *deep*. Complicated people make me ornery. I cannot pay attention to a conversation going on around me that is full of words I have not used since the SAT. So as this simple man began to pray for a woman named Gail at a healing service, I began to consider how God might view her blindness. Could her need quite possibly be a simple matter for Him?

We had decided as a church family to hold a service in which we would pray for people with physical problems. Many of us had been spending a lot of time in the gospels, and we had begun to wonder what would happen if we prayed for people the way Jesus did. We set out to find the answer. I have to admit, though, that I felt trepidation during the weeks leading up to the first healing service. I remember having conversations with my friends that went like this:

> *Friend:* "What are you going to preach about at the healing service?"
>
> *Me:* "I have no idea, and I've never been more nervous about anything in my life."

I laugh now when I look back at my trepidation. The only healing service I knew of was when a flashy fellow pressed someone's forehead with the palm of his hand and shouted, "Be healed in the name of *Je*-sus!"

But our service was not at all like that. It was inviting, warm and fun. Gail's friends helped her make her way to the front of the church, and I prayed gently for her. She said that she felt tingling in her face. Then God healed her right there on the spot. I did not jump around. (Other people did.) I did not throw snakes on the floor or twirl like a madman. I did not call attention to the situation at all.

Except that I was smiling. Until that moment, I had never thought I could pray and see someone get better. Maybe a headache here and there—but blindness? No way. When Gail's doctor examined her later, he could not believe what she said had happened in order for her to see. It made no sense to him.

Granted, I was as surprised as anyone. But then I began to consider, *Why don't we see more things like this?* That night energized my relentless pursuit of Jesus Christ and what He actually taught about the Kingdom.

A lot of things have happened since that service years ago when I prayed for Gail. It has been fun, scary, confusing and always adventurous. And it has been nothing like what I expected when I first started following Christ.

## Strange Happenings

I gave my life to Jesus Christ when I was twelve years old. I was sitting in my bedroom at 35 Prestwick Court in Spartanburg, South Carolina. There was no worship band or youth revival speaker. There were no goose bumps or visions. I did not even fully understand what I was doing, but I knew I simply needed Jesus.

Earlier that day, I had been listening to some men in our church describe their own journeys with God, and they had me thinking. I am not going to lie; I did not want to go to hell. A guest evangelist had previously scared me out of my mind. Thus, I was processing the idea of "knowing Jesus," but also the reality of going to hell for all of eternity if I did not give my life to Him.

Was my decision to accept Jesus driven by fear? Absolutely. It was years later, during counseling, before I realized this. Yet even though I could not describe what I was sensing, I knew that I needed to give Jesus my life. I knew that I was incomplete without being surrendered to Him. So I said out loud, "I want to give my life to You. Be my Savior."

The change in me was real. I read my Bible. I began preaching to my friends. I went to seminary and pastored college students. I traveled and spoke at churches and conferences. These were good years, but something was missing.

One night in a hotel room in San Angelo, Texas, I finally despaired of not seeing anything in my life that smelled and felt like the book of Acts. I was preaching to two thousand teenagers attending Youth Summer Camp, and after one session I went back to my hotel room and had it out with God.

I took my Bible and shook it at the heavens. I kept shouting, "There has to be more, God! All I do is preach to people that You want them with You in heaven forever!" I felt as though I was about to explode.

In my opinion, desperation does not make God move, but it does light a fire in your own belly so that you chase Him and His truth harder than you ever have. As the Bible tells us, when you seek Him with your whole heart, you find Him.

That night, I heard a voice tell me to turn on the television. I turned it on and flipped up two channels to a documentary in progress about a man named Reinhard Bonnke. I had never heard of him. The documentary talked about someone who had been raised from the dead in Africa. I remember feeling shocked as I watched it.

Remember, I had just finished screaming at God, "Why don't I ever see miracles like those in the book of Acts?" As I watched, transfixed, my heart leaped inside my chest. Finally, I had evidence that the things I longed for were possible. I had known for years that Stephen, Peter, John, Philip and Paul saw heaven change their natural-realm circumstances, but until that moment I had never heard of anyone doing anything like that in the here and now.

Sitting down under the weight of this revelation, I considered that perhaps it was possible for me to experience what this evangelist was experiencing. I sensed that I was about to know a lot more of God.

But there was a problem: How could I go about this discovery? Where did I even start? I really did not want to be viewed as some sort of a crazy man seeking attention. I was torn because even though I had a calling on my life, I have never been the type who stands out in the crowd in matters of faith. There is no fish on my car or Christian T-shirt in my closet. I love normal things like books and eating too much spaghetti.

This was before I knew that one can be natural and walk in the ways of the Kingdom at the same time. In the days that followed, I realized that I was scared to death that my friends and those to whom I was speaking would think that I had embraced whacked-out theology. And, honestly, I was scared to death that I might. The last thing I wanted to do was fall off the deep end into water where I had no business swimming.

## Reality Check

During this time I met well-known teacher and author Jack Deere. As I read his book *Surprised by the Voice of God*, I began to understand that I could actually walk with God in the way that my heart wanted. Jack was a respected scholar and seminary professor—someone I really trusted. I had just finished my seminary education, and I never want to check my brain at the door.

Thus, since I was curious about the life of Jesus, I came up with a plan. I stuck my head into the gospel of John for what seemed like a million hours and said, "Jesus, I'm all Yours. Show me what You want me to see—even if it ruins my life." I tell people all of the time that they should be careful about what they pray for. If I had known what it would cost me to pray that way, I might have been less inclined to mean it.

The book of John and the other gospels took hold of me. One day I hope to sit down with Peter, Andrew, John and some of the others and ask, "What was it like? I won't say anything to anybody—just be honest with me." I cannot imagine what it was like for them. A normal guy from nowhere came onto the scene and said, "Before Abraham was, I AM," and then started doing bizarre things.

Can you imagine being one of Jesus' birth brothers or sisters? There is no way in the world you and I would have believed Him. No one expected the Savior of the world to live in a backwoods town and pretty much be inconspicuous for thirty years.

Take a moment and imagine the following scenario. Joseph is sitting with his family over a meal and says to his young son James, "What do you want to do when you grow up, son?"

James replies, "You know, Dad, I've been thinking. I would like to be a part of the family business one day. I love working with wood, and I could see myself doing that for a long time."

Joseph smiles, and then turns to his eldest daughter. "What do you see yourself doing one day, honey?"

Looking at Mary, she answers, "I would absolutely love to be just like Mom. I want to take care of my family and help raise Jehovah-fearing children."

Mary then turns to Jesus and asks, "Sweetheart, what do You see Yourself doing when You get older?"

Jesus looks at her and says, "I plan on representing a government and establishing true concepts of My Father as I perform signs, wonders, healings and miracles in a twenty-four-mile radius of where we are now. I also see Myself recruiting an intimate group of followers who will learn from Me and then take My message all over the world by passing down the things I share with them. I sense that My Father will release His Spirit after I go rejoin Him. I'm about to do things that will make you stare into space, but what is really fun is that millions of others will be trained to do the same works I will do. I can't wait. Would you please pass the matzos?"

I have never seen one second of one day that can match the intensity of watching God in the flesh walk on water or tell dead people to get up. It is fairly easy for us today to think of Jesus doing those unusual things, but what about the others with Him? We, from our perspective, know the whole story; we can read the book of Revelation before we read the four gospels. But not them. A man showed up from Nazareth and taught the most controversial message the world has ever heard. I wonder what a fisherman thought when a Jewish Rabbi said, "Go tell people about My Daddy's Kingdom and raise the dead." And they actually did this.

I have been watching *The Gospel of John* (a movie produced by Philip Saville) with my kids. I double dog dare you to put down your presuppositions and watch that movie. Watch it over and over and notice how much it stretches your religious mind. The more I watch and listen to it (the script is a word-for-word version of John's gospel), the more I question what in the world I believe.

For most of my life, my Christianity has been defined by what I am *not doing*. I thought I was good with God because

I did not have any gross sins in my life. But when I read how Jesus operated and how He taught His followers to do the same things, I find myself gravitating toward what I *can do*.

The more I meditate on the gospel of John, the more I have come to believe that we have really tamed down our King, and made His message way too safe. Maybe that is because we want to be balanced. Try telling that to Jesus. If you had been His disciple and had told Him that you wanted to live a balanced life with a balanced theology, He would have said, "That's nice. If you want to follow Me, you must eat My flesh and drink My blood." Imagine how that went over in an Orthodox synagogue.

Why are we so obsessed with calming Jesus down? When it comes to the supernatural, most Christians who call themselves *disciples* say, "Let's make sure we focus on the main thing." This sounds wonderfully spiritual but is actually laced with the fear of man. Can you imagine what Jesus would have said to us if we had told Him: "Jesus, stop doing Your Father's works and focus on the main thing"?

Jesus did three things while He was here. He preached the Kingdom, healed the sick and cast demons out of people. Yet, how easy it is to find thriving churches—particularly in America—that do none of those three? I cannot go on living as though that is okay. I do not want to be a part of a church that can make it without the Holy Spirit. I do not want a master's degree in leadership and strategy and get to the point where I can lead others, if I do not have the fresh fire of the Father. The reason I love praying for the impossible is that I cannot take credit for it. I want to be a part of a movement that continues to say, "It had to be the Father. It just had to be."

I got to the point in my relationship where I just could not take it anymore. It was not enough for me to read about Him and preach truths that He taught. I wanted to see at least some of the things that Jesus saw. I wanted my life to have at least some resemblance to His.

## Our Spiritual Forebears

I know that "spiritualizing" our faith is only one reason that we fail to see the supernatural in our lives. Another reason— the main reason—is that most of us at least once have prayed sincerely, even earnestly, for a particular need—and nothing happened. Some of us have stored great libraries of doubt and disappointment.

Another reason we hesitate to go after the Kingdom whole-heartedly is that we see many abuses—yes, sadly, in the Church. This leads Christians to feel that attempts to see the Kingdom manifest on earth can open the door for extreme or dangerous beliefs.

Another reason is that we often acknowledge that God *can* heal, but we are not sure He always *wants* to. The fear of presumption overrides our confidence in His character.

These realities are far too prevalent. We all have painful questions that we plan to ask God when we enter heaven. Even so, I believe that a day is coming very, very soon when we will see more and more churches embrace the super-natural. I have a picture in my mind of two college students talking. One says to another, "What do you mean you go to a church that never sees our Father's works manifest? I haven't heard of a church like that in ten years."

Some of you reading this probably think that I am out in left field to suggest something like this. I would have thought the same thing a few years ago, but now I have seen and heard too much to think it is impossible. I am not talking here about the testimony of someone who lives in a country that I cannot pronounce. I am talking about a friend who is a dentist and sees the Kingdom manifest in his office on a regular basis as he prays for the broken. I am talking about countless others like him. These are normal, everyday people who are not famous, nor do they care to be.

I love stories of the saints of old who saw the impossible. Yes, I know that Hebrews 11 tells us of saints who never saw their Goliaths struck down. Trust me, I hear that. Keep reading and you will find that I am not a pie-in-the-sky person who thinks everything on planet earth is nice and tidy. The people who never saw victories are heroes in my book, but just as I do not ignore them, I also cannot throw away the stories of those who actually did see the impossible happen.

How in the world did Shamgar kill six hundred Philistines with an ox-goad? I have no idea, but if the impossible is possible, I want to do it, too. The Bible tells the stories of tons of Shamgars: Esther, Moses, Abraham, Deborah, Ehud, Peter, Noah, Aaron, Mary, John, Barnabas, Stephen and Timothy are but a small sampling of the people who saw God make the impossible happen through them.

I want to be like them. I want to see impossible things become possible in my life. I get excited when I read about Elijah calling down fire or Peter telling a dead child to wake up.

Now, granted, not one of us is Abraham or Moses or Elijah. But before we jump to the conclusion that we are not qualified to do amazing things like opening blind eyes, we need to take a closer look at how truly messed up many of our biblical heroes were.

I was encouraged my whole young adult life to consider the faith of Noah, and how he built an ark in the midst of scrutiny and criticism. But no one ever told me that Noah got off the boat and got drunk, and then got naked. (Imagine that felt-board lesson in Vacation Bible School.)

Or take Abraham. He is the father of millions and has been commended by generations for his faith. Yet if you examine his life closely, you find that he was no goodie-two-shoes. Abraham lied about Sarah being his wife to save his own hide not once but twice.

And what about Peter? Peter is the one with whom Jesus entrusted the Church after He went to be with His Father. Yet when you look at Peter's life and see his impetuousness and his intermittent lack of faith, you have permission to attempt what Peter attempted.

Let's be honest. If Peter's shadow could make someone whole, then perhaps through the power of the Holy Spirit we are capable of more than we think. If people's inadequacies could keep them from moving in power, then no one but Jesus would do great things. Perhaps it is possible to be as tangled as a tackle box and still see the impossible happen.

## Our Turn

Those heroes are gone now; it is our turn. That is why I get excited when I hear stories of people just like you and me who are seeing the same things our heroes saw. These are everyday people walking through their own normal problems with tiny faith and producing huge outcomes.

Think about this: Many of us who think that the impossible is not within our grasp are the same people who believe that one day we will leave our bodies and shoot off into heaven. How can we be sure? We believe this by faith. Then why not use that same type of childlike faith to say, "God, we have no idea how this all works, but we want to see You do fun, weird, miraculous stuff through us." Jesus continues to show me that I will miss 100 percent of the shots that I never take.

Again, I am not saying this as someone without pain. My journals are full of questions and hurt. Henri Nouwen was my literary mentor for a long season. I have agreed with Philip Yancey and preached that we all have our disappointments with God. But I cannot help asking why so many of us live our lives without the victories that our biblical ancestors experienced. If we say that we are children of a Father who props up His feet on the moon, then might our lives resemble something close to supernatural?

The night we prayed for Gail, I knew the answer was yes. I also knew that I had no idea what was in store for me.

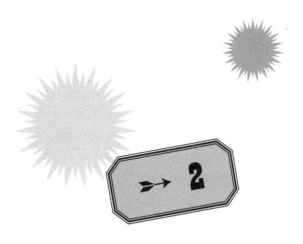

# Odd Teaching
# from an Odd Rabbi

I tend to do things in the extreme. At this point in my life I have stopped trying to figure out why and instead just go with it. The other day, for example, I bought a Vitamix. A Vitamix is a supercharged blender that could juice a tennis shoe. I figured that I needed to get back into juicing. Not only is it healthy, it is cool. I have bought cars for less than I spent on my Vitamix. My wife asked me what I paid for the Vitamix and I replied, "I love you, babe. I really do. How was your day?"

How could I not buy the Vitamix? Here is what happened. I went to Costco and watched a man demonstrate the Vitamix Terminator Superhero Heaven blender. I was hooked. This guy made ice cream from kale that tasted better than my favorite flavor at Baskin-Robbins.

And besides that, for some reason I have always been drawn to juicing. Let me take you back to 2005. I turned on the television one night, and this lady was talking about fasting for better health through juicing. She was going on and on about a drink to help your body detoxify called the Master Cleanser. Everything inside of me said, *Do it, fatty.* I had never been more than three hours without eating, much less ten days, which the cleanser required.

But I could not turn away. I decided to do the Master Cleanser juice detoxification. My conversation with my wife went something like this: "Hey, babe, I'm not going to eat for ten days. I'm going to drink lemon juice with red cayenne pepper and Grade B organic maple syrup."

Wendy looked at me and said, "Chad, it is so hard to take you seriously. Is this like the time you told me that you were going to train for the Ironman competition in Hawaii, or the time you thought God was calling you to hike the Appalachian Trail for six months to raise money?"

This time I actually followed through. That Master Cleanser juice detoxifier almost killed me. I lost nine hundred pounds in ten days. I happened to be in the Cincinnati airport on Day Eleven as I was coming off of the fast. I had not had anything but that miserable drink for ten long days, and wanted orange juice so badly that I would have cut off a finger to get it.

Well, apparently, I drank my orange juice at the airport too fast. I was walking to the gate to catch my flight, when all of a sudden I had a feeling come over me like an internal attack by colonic fighter jets. You know what I am talking about. It is that moment when you realize that you have one minute to get to the bathroom or your life will change forever.

I sprinted toward the bathroom like that Jamaican guy who outruns everybody. Jesus saved the situation, because I made it just in time. I did not think it was odd as I ran into the restroom that nobody else was in there. Of course, I was not really thinking at the time. But I did think it was odd when I came out of the stall and three women turned to stare at me.

Have you ever been in an awkward moment when you had no idea what to do? All I could say was, "I'm sorry, and I am not a pervert." I jetted to my gate with my insides rumbling and my head held low in shame. It was a moment when I was using all of my resources just to get my bearings. I kept thinking, *How did I get myself into this?*

## Can You Imagine?

I promise you that Peter, Andrew, John and the other disciples had many moments when they were asking the same thing: *How did we get ourselves into this?* I can picture Matthew saying to Bartholomew, "Hey, Bart, can you explain to me how that eyeball just grew back into that guy's eye socket?"

Those of us who follow Jesus today have lost the sense that it is normal to feel awkward about some of the things Jesus expects us to do. We should be pondering most of the time, *How did I get myself into this?* Trust me: The fact that I am talking about these things does not mean that I am never caught off guard. I am stunned quite often.

Think for starters about what we believe as disciples of Christ. We believe that a little boy was born in a little town called Bethlehem to peasant parents. He grew up in a normal family with normal siblings. When He was twelve years old, He found His way into a religious setting and talked with such authority that He impressed the religious leaders.

This twelve-year-old named Jesus then disappeared for eighteen years. We hear not a peep about Him in Scripture during this time in His life. Then He turned thirty, went down to the riverbank and got baptized by His cousin. When He came up out of the water, a visual concept of the Holy Spirit rested on His shoulder. This man left the river and began a ministry that would last only about 1,200 days.

During these 1,200 days, He talked about things that no one had ever talked about before. Jesus talked about His Father in heaven a lot. When He was not talking about His Father and His Father's Kingdom, He was healing people. He also cast out demons. And what is even more astonishing is that He taught His followers to do the same.

Can you imagine how strange it would have been to watch this happen? Just imagine yourself standing beside Him when He told a corpse to come out of a grave. The man he called to had been dead for four days. Let that sink in. Picture Lazarus walking out as you stare at him.

Jesus left that scene, and in a short time He was hanging on a cross. And just when you think it could not get any stranger, this man who died a criminal's death—with people watching, remember—was all of a sudden alive and well again. A few days later He barbequed fish for His disciples.

Fast-forward a couple thousand years, and His disciples are still talking about Him. You can travel almost anywhere today and realize that most of the world is wide open to the

Father's works. You can see and hear stories of the same types of things He did on earth.

But somehow, many Christians, particularly in America, still cannot fathom the odd lifestyle that this odd Rabbi wants us to embrace. Some people who believe in Him simply want to avoid a hot, miserable place for all eternity. Others say that they want to serve Him. But what does that mean? What does that look like?

Let me ask this question another way: If we had followed Jesus while He was on the earth, what would He have asked us to do? Seriously, what would this odd rabbi have expected of us if we were literally by His side? The only answer I can come up with is that He would have asked us to do what He asked His other disciples to do, even if it led to some awkward moments that left us wondering how we ever got into such a strange situation.

## Believe or Follow?

Well, then, what did Jesus ask His disciples to do? In the gospels, you read often that Jesus said, "Follow Me." You do not read nearly as much that He said, "Believe in Me." Personally, I think that every demon in hell believes in Jesus. I doubt any of them are following Him.

This is why it can be pretty scary if I am confident in doctrines and paradigms that bear no resemblance to what following Jesus looked like a couple of millennia ago. In many of our churches, Jesus is a secret. I have been around a lot of people who know more about Abraham, Job and Moses than they do about the One who holds it all together.

As God began to open my eyes to the gospels themselves, I realized that this was true of me. I sat by myself one day in my backyard and wrote this in my journal: "I'm not so sure I really know Jesus." I preach and write about this man for a living, and I was saying that I barely knew Him. At that point, I started asking hard questions of myself.

I love the gospels. I admit it. They give me a peek at three years in the history of the earth when an unknown from nowhere flipped the world upside down. And if I am calling myself this man's disciple, then there should be some similarities in my life to what I find in those four books. When my life does not look a lot like His, I feel convicted. It can be uncomfortable to compare yourself to your leader.

Yet that is the predicament I have been in for the last ten years. When I turned thirty, I asked myself, *Why do you love Him so much and yet not see the things He saw while He was here?* I have grown tired of trying to manage my own spiritual formation. I want things that I cannot explain to happen in my life on a daily basis. I want heaven to be attracted to my life in the way it was attracted to Jesus' life.

A few years ago, I decided to deal with the dead plant in my office. I had just read how Jesus cursed a fig tree and it died. I decided to tell the plant to live. It was not *almost* dead; it was dead. I felt like an idiot, but I looked right at the plant and told it to wake up in the name of Jesus. That was Friday afternoon. When I came back to the office on Monday, that plant looked brand-new. I began to wonder what else I had been missing.

I want to do life with people who feel water under our feet as we walk on it. I long to see storms settle down quickly because we tell them to. I want to see a Lazarus wake up so that I have to say, "Give him something to eat; he's hungry." I yearn to do the things my Master did while He was here. This is not because I want superpowers; this is because I want to follow Jesus.

If this makes you want to roll your eyes I completely understand. I used to roll my eyes when I heard people talk this way. But then I let the gospels start telling me what was normal.

And gradually, the more I hung around those four gospels, the more I felt a vortex pulling me into the life known as being His disciple. I have seen blind eyes open. I have seen deaf ears come unstopped. I have seen people freed from demonic entanglement. I have watched this play out in my life as I minister to others.

Is it sometimes awkward? Yes. Remember that the closer Jesus got to the cross, the fewer disciples He had. It just goes to show how much easier it is to believe in Jesus than it is actually to follow Him. John was the last man standing at the cross, which is why I find it interesting that he was the one called the Beloved Disciple. It is not easy to be a beloved disciple of Jesus.

Yet how can we be passionate about Jesus and not do what He spent most of His time doing? His Father's works—praying for the sick and broken—were central to Jesus' ministry. He did not start a denomination, charismatic or otherwise; He released the Kingdom. So what would He and the disciples say about the current state of the Church? I think the King would encourage His disciples to accept His love and engage in His works. The Greek word for *disciple* is *mathetes*, and it means "one who learns." The early disciples did not just learn who Jesus was—they learned to do the things He did.

I believe the Father wants to look upon a world right now full of His children who act like Jesus. Even though it is not always easy, even though we may wonder sometimes how we got where we are, this is still what I read so much about in those four little books. I have a feeling Matthew, Mark, Luke and John would say the same thing if they came to town for a conference.

This is not a new idea of discipleship; it is an old idea of simply following our leader.

## Look-Alikes

One of the most wonderful things I hear on a regular basis is this: "Welcome to Moe's." I hope you have had the opportunity to hear this for yourself by going to eat at a Moe's Southwest Grill. To me, these three words are just as wonderful as the sound of Santa's bells when I was a child going to the mall to sit in the big man's lap. There are not many demands I make on life, but I crave Mexican food. The smell of burritos and cheese dip can make me emotional.

On one of my weekly visits to Moe's, I looked at the pictures of famous people scattered around the room. I made a comment to my friend with me about Michael Jackson's picture. My buddy said, "That's not Michael Jackson. That's another guy who looks just like him." On closer inspection I saw that he was right. I could not believe that the people in those pictures looked so much like their superstar heroes.

My friend and I got into a conversation about those look-alike pictures and how they relate to the Kingdom. It is funny how the Holy Spirit can teach you something in an unlikely place. The conclusion we came to that day is that none of us should ever try to be anyone else. My goal is not to look like you, and your goal is not to look like me. One of the most freeing moments in my life was the day I finally became comfortable in my own skin. Being fully me is fun. Not everybody will like me, but my goal is to be who I truly am.

What does this have to do with the supernatural? Most people never attempt to walk in the ways of the power of the Kingdom because they presuppose that they will have to look like someone else. I am here to tell you that you can be fully yourself and see the Kingdom manifest.

Some of us, for instance, are incredibly introverted. That is no problem at all. At our church, people who are very introverted pray regularly for the sick and broken. They see breakthrough quite often. Recently, for example, two unassuming and quiet women prayed for a woman with scoliosis, and she experienced the Kingdom.

I, on the other hand, am extroverted. If I went on a silent retreat for a week, I would probably try to cut off my pinkie with a spoon. Writing this book has been tough for me because I have spent so much time alone. Praying for people is no big deal for me because I am energized by being around others.

We are all different, and that is a beautiful thing. We can celebrate each other's differences as we become all that our leader calls us to be. There will be times when we will wonder how we ever got into the predicaments we find ourselves in, but the question remains: Are we still learning from the One the disciples learned from?

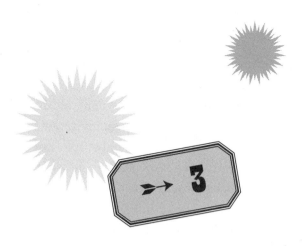

# Southern Charm

I grew up in your typical southern town dominated by hospitality, high school football and a Southern Baptist church on every corner. It probably comes as no surprise that my brother, sister and I grew up Baptist. We went to a huge Baptist church, and I loved it. Dr. Alastair Walker was a hero to me, and I am still proud of my memories as a young man there. But even as a child, I felt as though something was amiss in my spiritual formation. The more Bible stories I heard, the more I started to think, *Why don't we see any of these things now?*

I remember sitting at our kitchen table one Sunday after church when I was twelve years old and asking my parents, "Why do we spend so much time talking about going to heaven when we die? How come we never see people get healed?" My dad stared at me as if I had just said that I was going out on my own to raise catfish in Mississippi.

He probably concluded that I was confused. I was not confused; I was mad. I was tired of focusing on avoiding hell and spending forever in heaven. Even as a young kid I used to say, "Who in the world would say no to an invitation to miss hell and enjoy heaven forever?" I remember an evangelism course in which we were taught to ask the sole question, "If you died right now, where would you go?" A lot of what I was hearing was fear-based. At least that was my interpretation; undoubtedly that was not the case at all times.

I have since come to realize that Jesus never asked that question. It helps me to think about it this way: God put Adam and Eve here on earth for a reason. He did not put them in heaven. If God had wanted Adam and Eve in heaven, He would have put them there instead of in the Garden. I am as excited about heaven as anyone else, but I cannot help but wonder why a lot of the pulpits in America spend more time focusing on going there instead of unleashing the Kingdom here.

This was the question on my heart at the kitchen table that day. I wondered why we hardly ever talked about miracles in the here and now. So next I asked my dad why no one ever did things the way Jesus did. I remember Mom stepping in and saying that I was asking good questions. That assuaged me for the time being, and I moved on like any other twelve-year-old. I got up from the table and went about my business of playing football in the yard and asking God for a pretty girlfriend.

As I got older, I kept asking the same questions—which led me to some interesting places: encountering angels, healing sick people, watching people receive deliverance from demons, meeting a voodoo temple leader who gave her life to Jesus Christ, having open visions and hearing God's voice when I am not even praying. If that seems strange to you, then get in line: It seems strange to me, too.

But it is becoming less strange. The more I study the Bible, the more I wonder what normal is. For a long time my biggest fear of doing all that Jesus wants me to do was that people would write me off as a nutcase. You might have that fear, too. If so, like me you have probably wondered at times if the cost of raising the flag of surrender to a King we cannot see is really worth it. I have decided that my answer to that is yes. It is not always easy, but it is always worth it.

## Following Our Leader

If you spent any time with me, you would soon realize that there is nothing fancy about me. I am not cool. I have never thought that I know everything. I have struggled with depression, panic attacks and insecurity. I have been on medication, wondered if God really loves me and entertained enough thoughts of unworthiness to choke a goat.

Through all of it, though, I have grown convinced of one thing: I am now as clean as Jesus Christ in my Father's eyes. And that knowledge makes me convinced of one other thing: They are both looking and waiting to see if I will do everything they have commanded me to do—and that is not solely to tell people that they can go to heaven when they die, as important as that message is.

More probably, though, following Jesus means to preach the Kingdom of God and heal the sick. Luke 9:2 is pretty clear that this is what Jesus sent His disciples out to do. This might make us uncomfortable, but we will be okay. At some point we have to stop ignoring what He told us to do. There are people all around us who are dying to hear the message of the Kingdom and experience its power.

Why do I think that He wants us to do these things? Because it does not make sense that Jesus would have different expectations of His disciples "today" than He had of His disciples "yesterday." If Jesus is eternally the same, has His mission changed? Has discipleship changed?

Peter was messed up emotionally. I can relate to him. Many of the disciples jilted Jesus at His most important moment. Those guys had their own problems, just as we have ours. Yet in the middle of our messiness, we find the call to do the things that our leader did: preach the Kingdom of God and heal the sick. We do this not only because we need His help every day of our lives, but also because doing these things brings glory to the Father.

One day a man brought his son to Jesus' disciples because a demon kept throwing the boy into fires. The disciples tried, but they could do nothing to help. At this revelation, Jesus expressed His displeasure with them. He fussed at His disciples (not the "unbelievers" following them) for their unbelief because they could not cast the demon out (see Luke 9:41).

Contrary to Jesus' clear intent and actions in this story, I have heard many pastors over the years talk about God receiving "glory" from the misery of His children. Undoubtedly, you have, too. But imagine one of those pastors among Jesus' disciples. Picture Jesus present as this disciple fails to help a young child who is possessed by a demon. Then imagine the disciple looking at Jesus and saying solemnly, "May God get all of the glory for this boy's torment."

Jesus would probably respond with something like, "My Father gets glory when we do His works. Bring the child to Me."

How is it, then, that thousands upon thousands of people today believe that God gets glory if His children are sick or tortured? I have strong feelings about this because I was given similar "encouragement" at a time of tragedy in my life, as I will explain a little later.

Some people hold on to an even deadlier variation of this message, claiming that Jesus sends torment into people's lives in order to teach them a lesson. The net result of these bad theologies is that we hardly hear any talk in the Church on the supernatural for today—and we hear a lot of talk about getting to heaven where we will finally find relief from our pain and trauma.

If it were possible for Jesus to get sick, I think He would have an upset stomach regarding what the Church is saying (or not saying) about these things. If He fussed at His boys for not living out His Kingdom message, I cannot imagine what He would say to us who can experience the presence of the Holy Spirit.

Well, maybe I can.

I was preparing to preach at Heritage Church in Moultrie, Georgia, one Sunday morning. I was in a side room sitting in God's presence and focusing on my sermon. A man from Moultrie named Roy Reeves had been a significant father figure in my life, and I was thanking the Lord for his influence. Then out of nowhere I heard these words inside of me: *Chad, I'm tired of you preaching old revelation. I need you to dig in and draw closer to Me. There is a lot more I want to show you. Get busy.*

I am not going to lie; Jesus hurt my feelings. Here I was getting ready to tell a bunch of people about how much God loved them, and Jesus fussed at me. I wanted to say to the Lord, "Do You not realize that people's number-one fear is speaking in public? I'm sitting here trying to focus on my sermon and all I hear is how I am preaching old revelation."

Here was the problem, though: Jesus was right. He sets the bar high for His disciples. That is not just my opinion; that is what I find in the gospels. He loves us, but He has high expectations of us as well.

Frankly, if I were leading, I would not pick me to be part of the team. I would find someone who has his or her act together. But Jesus is funny that way. He loves to call the broken to help the broken. I think one of the reasons our church sees so many people healed is because we know what it feels like to be broken ourselves.

I have learned—and I hope my story will show you—that God does not giggle with excitement when we stay in brokenness. Jesus wants us, His disciples, to bring His Kingdom power to this broken world. He wants us to let people know that it is actually possible to be whole. I know that this can happen for you and those you love because it happened for me. It starts as we learn to wait.

"Action in waiting" sounds like a contradiction, but that is because we have so little understanding of what it means to wait on God. Let me show you what I mean.


## Waiting on God

I used to tell people (including myself) all the time, "Just wait on God." But when Jesus showed me His idea of "waiting," my little mind was stunned.

*Wait* in English is a passive word, but Jesus' idea is active. Think of it this way. If you go to a nice steakhouse for dinner and your waiter—the one who is "waiting" on you—never comes to your table, you would be perturbed. A waiter's job is to be attentive to the one he or she is serving. A good waiter will assess what you want him or her to do and then try to please you by doing it: "How would you like your steak cooked? May I get you more tea? Will you be having dessert tonight?"

The idea of waiting on God, in other words, is not waiting for a bus but waiting on a table. We might call it relentless southern hospitality. It means diving headfirst into the pleasure of serving Him, and we start that process by learning more about what He likes. I have found again and again that the more I "wait on" God by doing the things He expects me to do, the more I see my heavenly homeland affect this realm. Recently, for instance, I felt led to go on an extended fast. I had had a random encounter with God, and He had told me point-blank to do this. Even though fasting seems passive, it really is not. Fasting is active waiting.

If we will begin to study the art of what it means to "wait" on Him, we will see more of the Kingdom manifesting in our lives. It is interesting how in the natural realm you get stuffed when you eat a lot of food. In the unseen realm, however, it seems as though the more we feast on Him the hungrier and hungrier we become for more of who He is.

Once I began looking at discipleship this way, I realized that there was no turning back. It means, among other things, that I ask a lot of questions. Do you have questions? Most people do. Mine go like this:

Why did Jesus tell us to call God "Father"?

Why did Jesus feel more comfortable being around thieves and hookers than He did religious folk?

Why did the multitudes flock to this man, and why did the religious establishment hate Him?

Why do so many people today despise being around Christians but love who Jesus is?

Why do so many people who call themselves "disciples" not do what Jesus commanded them to do?

I am amazed when I hear conversations or read the words of disciples of Jesus who are still processing whether or not the gifts are ours today. Perhaps in the middle of our service to Jesus, we will find that our Father is more than willing to do through us what He did through His Number-One Son. I find it interesting that Jesus never preached healing or signs and wonders. He never preached prosperity or deliverance. He just preached the Kingdom of His Father, and blessing flooded people like a river from heaven. He called them His Father's works (see John 10:37). I like that.

Jesus had one goal: Present His Father and His Father's Kingdom to the world and provide a way for us to reconnect to that same Father and Kingdom. Jesus told His boys in the Upper Room that nobody could get to His Father but through Him (see John 14:6).

For me, getting to know Jesus' Father has saved my life. There were times when I never thought I would get to the point where I could say that. Life is strange. In a bit, I will tell you why I spent many years hating God. Now I desire to serve Him solely because I love Him with every fiber of my being. He has been good to me, and that is why I will never go back. It is my desire and pleasure to wait on Him.

## Group of Holy Misfits

Sometimes when I share my stories of waiting on God, people look at me as if to say, "You are really weird." Some people call our church weird. The other day I was having lunch with a friend. We were talking about this very thing, and he suggested I look up the definition of the word *weird*. When I did, things came into focus. It means "unearthly, uncanny and involving the supernatural." I like that a lot. From now on, when people ask me what I am, I plan to say that I am weird.

This is mainly because I am not a citizen here. My home is in another land. Since I am from there and headed back there, it should be normal for me to experience weird, supernatural things here.

In the past year, I have had the opportunity to share life with men from various backgrounds, interests and religious upbringings. Our group consists of computer gurus, landscapers, business owners, international business consultants, fitness coaches, video technicians and entrepreneurs. We go to church together, eat together, laugh together and share struggles and victories. We are all very different yet very much the same. Our commonality lies in our desire to wait on God.

Thus, this group of holy misfits has set out on a quest to find the God of the Bible. We tear through books, papers, articles, conversations, times of prayer and moments of reflection. We meet for hours at a time in search of one thing:

the knowledge of who God is and how His Kingdom operates. Every one of these normal men lives the norm for disciples of Jesus Christ. As we preach the Kingdom and pray for the broken, I sense that many people are aching for what our weird group has found together, because we are finding God the Father.

I prize my Father all the more because of the journey I am on. As I have already hinted, the story of the supernatural in my life runs alongside the story of pain and difficulties. Perhaps you have known times of hardship. Few of us have not. As I tell you my story in the next three chapters, I pray that it will help you want to wait on God relentlessly. That is where you will find answers for all of the questions that fill your heart.

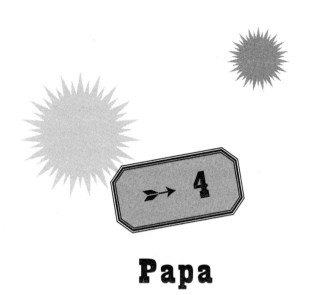

# Papa

Bill Norris was my hero. He was a hero to others, too, because he was an army major in World War II. People who knew Bill said he was a man's man. I like that idea—a common man who could relate to anyone.

Bill Norris was my grandfather, hero and friend. It is funny how a five-year-old can build a relationship with an adult that reaches to the cellular level of his emotions. That is what happened between us. It seems as though grandparents can reach a child in a way parents cannot.

I was convinced that my grandfather could do anything. One time Papa and Mama Jane took me to the Okefenokee Swamp. "Chad," Papa said, "years ago I wrested an alligator to his back and tickled him." I remember thinking, *A man who can tickle an alligator is the coolest man in the world. My Papa is bigger than life.* Even though he was kidding, I loved it.

The other day my nine-year-old son, Sam, said, "Dad, remember when your Papa turned that alligator over and tickled its belly?"

I said, "I sure do, Sammy. He tickled that thing to death."

Papa took me with him to play golf, fish and simply be with other adults. I felt loved and respected, and I liked that. I used to sit on the bathroom floor while he shaved. I watched and wondered what it felt like to be a superhero. When I sat with him in his big green leather recliner, I felt like the safest person in the world. When my parents would drop me off at Papa and Mama Jane's house for a visit my blood would race through my veins because I was about to be treated like a king.

Even now, years later, I can remember the smell of their house. I can remember his deep voice as he chatted with Mama Jane. They sat on the porch in two rocking chairs in the evenings. My parents still have those rockers, and when we visit them, I go outside and rock and think about those days.

Now, I fully realize that God puts grandparents on this earth to spoil their grandkids. My children now go wild when my father—"Big Jim"—comes walking into the house. You can hear them yell "Big Jim! Big Jim!" from a mile away. I see Papa in my dad.

Papa and Mama Jane lived in Thomson, Georgia, and so Thomson became my own little Narnia. It was a world of bliss. But on September 15, 1977, my magical kingdom crumbled. My hero dropped dead of a heart attack. Suddenly, he was gone.

The next few times I visited his house I wandered in a maze of confusion. I kept asking, "Where is my Papa?

Somebody, tell me where my Papa is." I tried to run away to find where he was. I felt so alone. Hopeless. Detached. Little did I know that I would carry this pain for the next 25 years. As I got older it was like a nightmare I could not escape. A counselor later would put the word *trauma* on this event in my life.

We all have our "Papa" stories. It is hard to realize how tough life can be. The other night I was praying for someone who was struggling emotionally, and the Lord gave me an impression of Himself crying over her. I think that He cares more deeply about the things we go through than we can imagine. I will never forget the first time it dawned on me that Jesus *wept* when Lazarus died. Sometimes the only thing that gets us through tough days or seasons is the faith to realize that He weeps with us as we fight our battles.

## Confusion Multiplied

A well-meaning family friend finally stepped in with an answer to my question. She thought her words would give me comfort, but she poisoned my view of God for many years. In fact, it was decades before I could resolve my anger toward God.

"Chad," she said, "God needed a flower in His garden up in heaven."

I have no memory of the lady's name who said that to me. She was elderly and I am sure she thought she was helping. I have never blamed her for trying. But with those words, a painful belief about God was cemented within my soul: *Don't get too close to Big Bad God. If you do, He'll take what is closest to you. He'll teach you a lesson by "blessing" you with the death of someone you love.*

This is a theology—the same kind that Job's friends tried to talk him into—that many people hear in times of tragedy. It is a dangerous and deadly line of thinking. When I thought that it was true, I smoldered with anger.

Jesus Christ of Nazareth never made anyone suffer pain. He never killed anyone in His ministry. He never made anyone sick or tormented anyone with demons. Sometimes as I am ministering to others, I feel anguish at how many people believe that Jesus is the author of their misery, that He is looking down from heaven to see how He might rip their hearts out for their own good.

## What Heaven Sees

Think about it: How do you feel about the idea of God watching over you from heaven? Are you comfortable with it, or are you a little bit worried? I can think of all the times I have seen a preacher's eyes bulge out of his head as he described the imminent wrath of a ticked-off God. And I think I have heard at least a hundred times in the last ten years a variation of Isaiah 48:11, such as: "God will not share His glory with another—and that means you!"

There is a problem, though, with how that verse is being interpreted. Jesus gave us a very different idea in a prayer to His Father: "I have given them the glory that you gave me" (John 17:22).

Is that not one of the most shocking sentences you have read in a while? I am still processing what God is showing me in this area. There are times even now when I get on my face before Him because I am so amazed at what He has given me as a result of my being in Christ. The Gospel truly is the best news I have ever heard. Theology saved my life when I really started believing this. I used to take my wife's lipstick and write on our bathroom mirror, *Chad, God really does love you.* I would write passages about His love for me on note cards and read them over and over and over until I could actually sense the Word taking root in my heart.

Have you ever noticed grass growing through cement? Odd. Seed is powerful. When the Word of God began to grow in my heart, I started thinking differently.

The problem is not more information; the problem is having the courage to believe what He has already said. I am not guilty anymore. I am forgiven. Anyone who walks in the awareness of who he or she is in Christ can trigger insecurities in—and criticism from—others. But when we believe what that beautiful Book says about us, we put ourselves in a better position to receive His favor in our lives.

God keeps telling me that He wants me to grow in favor (see Luke 2:52). This past year, I have been exploring what that means. He keeps showing me that favor follows identity. If I do not know who I am in His eyes, it is very difficult to walk in the ways of His Kingdom. I cannot deny that as I have been attacking this concept, I have seen His favor manifesting in my life. Jesus was clear about seeking first the Kingdom and His righteousness; it follows that all of the other things will be added to us (see Matthew 6:33).

Our Father sees us as kings. He sees us clothed in purple. He expects us to say things like, "Who just defied the name of my God?" The supernatural realm invading the natural realm is disturbing only if we cannot grasp who we are: His disciples.

Jesus Christ never rejoiced in the deaths of people around Him. Instead, He told people to get up out of their coffins. If Jesus Christ was the perfect representation of the Father on earth (see Hebrews 1:3), and if, as Paul says, when we see Jesus we see God in action, then we can affirm that God does not "love" us into destruction. He desires wholeness.

## God in Action

A. W. Tozer said: "What comes into our minds when we think about God is the most important thing about us." It is alarming when you realize how important it is to think correctly about who He says you are. Hosea 4:6 tells us that what we do not know can destroy us. I have also come to realize that what we do know can set us free.

John 8:32 is the key to this whole process: "Then you will know the truth, and the truth will set you free." The only truth that will set us free is the truth we know to be true. In other words, the thoughts we have about ourselves as humans are not necessarily reality. Reality is defined by what the Father, Jesus and the Holy Spirit think. The word *Satan* in Hebrew means "accuser." The enemy loves to seduce us into contradicting the thoughts that God actually has toward us. Any thoughts that do not line up with God's Word do not come from God.

When Jesus began His ministry, He told the people to "repent" (see Matthew 4:17). The word for *repent* is *metanoia*, which means "change the way you think." When I learned to change the way I think, my life began to change. That is why I am passionate about what I do. Since Satan comes against us with lies, I find myself on a "truth mission" every time I minister. For the rest of my life I want to help people know the truth of who God is and how He sees His children.

I prayed for a woman at our church recently in one of our healing services, and she told me how another minister that very day had told her that God was receiving glory from her migraines.

I said to her, "Let me make sure I understand what you are saying. You are telling me that you think God is pleased and receiving glory by His beloved daughter having migraines?" Very gently I said to her, "Can you find one single passage when Jesus said anything like this? Did Jesus ever celebrate when someone was in physical pain?"

I then gave her a big hug and said, "Why don't we pray with the faith of a three-year-old and open our hearts to His love. Instead of waiting for some huge ball of faith to well up in you, why don't you just go for the faith of a mustard seed?"

Tears filled her eyes as I continued to talk to her, particularly when I mentioned the difference between relating to God only as "God" and not as "Father." I then prayed, and she was set free. Her migraine left. She was astonished. She could hardly believe it.

Now, I know what you might be thinking: *Listen, I love Jesus, but I'm not going down some wild charismatic trail.* Don't worry. Neither am I. If you could take a ride with me in my ancient minivan and hang out at, let's say, my son's football practice, you would be okay with the normalcy of my life. In other words, any regular person who truly believes you are who He says you are can see things like this happen. It is no big deal.

I think our Father gets glory when His children act like their Big Brother. I ask people all the time, "Do you think the Lord would help you if He were here in the flesh?" Only a couple of times have I heard someone say no.

When Kingdom citizens do their best to represent the Father and Jesus to someone in pain, and breakthrough does not come, they do not conclude, "It must be God's will for you to remain in your tortured state." Rather, they empathize with the person, acknowledging that even though Jesus never caused any physical, mental or emotional pain, this situation is still not yet changing. Sometimes the deepest thing you can do is weep with someone and say, "I am so sorry."

This is better than creating theologies to answer every question—or, worse, condemning a hurting person for having a lack of faith. Quite a few times over the past ten years, I have prayed for people and nothing happened. Instead of sprinting out the back door in order to avoid facing the failed expectations, I talk about how faith is messy. Condemning them or even condemning myself serves zero purpose.

I have found, though, that it is helpful simply to be present, authentic and vulnerable while admitting that I do not have all the answers. Trust me. I have a lot of questions that I plan on asking God one day.

## Dealing with Papa's Death

Twenty-five years after Papa's death, a counselor asked me, "Did you lose someone close to you when you were a child?"

That question hit me like a ton of bricks. I finally mourned him. I went to his grave and wrote him a long letter good-bye. At one point, with the help of my counselor, I found out how broken my heart had been.

Looking back on it now, losing Papa turned out to be the biggest catalyst for the biggest pursuit of my life. I wanted to know who God was and why He had killed my hero. I think I secretly wanted to find out how I could hurt God in the way that He had hurt me—since He was the one I was told was responsible.

Thus, any time someone said that God is loving, I rebelled against it. Even my decision to give my life to Jesus was more about not going to hell than forming an actual relationship with God. I think most of us get so consumed by our own messes that it is easier to navigate the pain we are in than fight for the freedom of territory we have never occupied. Maybe that is why Jesus asked that man who had been sick for 38 years this strange question: "Do you want to get well?" (John 5:6). Let that sink in for just a second. There is a price to pay for freedom. You have to be willing to admit you need help from someone else.

Jesus has the same purpose for all of our lives: to lead us to His Father. If I am not finding myself getting closer to His Father, I might not be following Jesus. The destination is always the same. Always. We all have different strengths, gifts and abilities but our destination is always toward the One who sent Jesus to earth in the first place.

One of my lifelong friends has now become my brother. His name is David, and he is the worship pastor at the church I serve. A while back we were talking and I said, "I have never known anyone in my life I have less in common with than you." David's computer probably cost more than both of my minivans put together. I love football; David knows nothing of the National Football League. I have no style; David has a pair of boots that could win a fashion contest. When I want to relax, I play golf. When David relaxes he drives two hours to look at art and eat chocolate truffles. If I wore one of his V-neck T-shirts, I would be arrested. So why in the world are we brothers? It is simple—we have the same Father.

Life is too short and precious to follow an illusion. When we begin connecting with the Father on an everyday basis, we will learn how passionate He is about heaven touching His earth through us. I have more questions than answers, but I can hang my hat on one thing for sure, and that is the reality that as my Father, He truly does care for me.

## "Thank You" Seems Trite

When I was in seminary, I was assigned to write a paper describing why I am thankful for Jesus. I should go write that paper again. If not for Jesus, I would have no shot at peace in any area of my life.

People fill their days with busyness to keep down the whisper in the back of their souls that says, *How are you in the eyes of God right now?* If we do not answer that question on this earth, we will answer it in the world to come. As for me, the reason I love my Savior so much is that He makes me clean in the eyes of God. I have never gotten over that revelation and I never will.

People are generally more familiar with stories about God striking people down (as in Leviticus 10) than they are with the Bible's invitation to come into the throne room any time we want (see Hebrews 4:16). I worship my God and give Him glory, but I also come to Him with confidence.

That chapter in Leviticus tells us of the time when Aaron's two sons (who had names like selections at a high-end taco restaurant) decided to visit God. Small problem: God had not invited them. So what did God do? He smoked them like a Thanksgiving turkey. Poof—they were gone. Can you imagine having an altar call at church and God killing everyone who comes forward? It happened to Nadab and Abihu. And they were sons of the high priest.

The Law was given as an instrument; grace came in the Person of Jesus Christ. Note the difference—*given* is different from *came*. Grace being a Person is a phenomenal concept. Can you imagine having God in the flesh stand beside you and not even know it? He is the One who said to that woman caught in the act of adultery, "Neither do I condemn you" (John 8:11). *God* said that to her. That is incredible to me.

Yet, it was not always like that. Nadab and Abihu were killed; we get to be held. Thank God for Jesus. When God inspects us now, He looks at His Son. I still cannot get over it. When God views a person who is in Christ, He views him or her through the blood of His own Son.

The fact that I can stand in the presence of Almighty God as a clean man is mind-boggling. Colossians 1:21–22 is a hall-of-fame passage in my life. I used to be alienated, dirty and pathetic, but not anymore. Now I am clean, forgiven and whole. He *likes* me.

I remember reading Martin Luther in seminary and hoping that one day I would have his revelation that God is not angry all of the time. Nothing will drive you crazy like the idea that God is ticked off at you. Jesus makes me sane. Jesus comes in and says, "Let Me take you to My Father. He's not as upset as you think He is."

One night Wendy and the kids were off visiting family and I was home by myself. I was listening to some Celtic worship music and soaking in the presence of the Lord. For whatever reason, I decided to light some candles; I have no idea why. I turned the lights off, and by the gentle glow of candlelight said, "Lord, I want to tell You what I'm struggling with."

Now what I am about to tell you will infuriate a religious person. I am just telling you what happened. Before I could even finish my sentence the Lord said to me, *Chad, you are funny. What are you doing?*

During that time of my life, Jesus seemed to go out of His way to shatter my view of what I thought God was like. Here I was trying to be serious and talk to God about my shortcomings, and He just smiled.

I am telling you: He is not as uptight as many believe He is. He loves to champion who we are in Him and call us to the deeper waters of growth and spiritual formation. It is like the time God called Gideon a "mighty warrior" (Judges 6:12). Gideon was nowhere near being a mighty warrior. It is as though God saw what he could become and called him into that greater maturity.

The night Jesus told me that I was amusing Him, what I really heard Him say was, "Chad, I am not obsessed with your shortcomings. Spend time with Me and focus on who you are in Me." He has done that time and time again in my life. In fact, I seem to get this revelation about once a year. He continues to push me to discover who I am in Him.

Sometimes I pray for people after I have just come out of a moment of "intense fellowship" with my wife—the kind of "intense fellowship" that starts with a difference of opinion and includes loud voices. When I show up at our healing service after those moments, I say to myself as I walk through the doors, "I pray on the basis of who He is in me and not on myself. I will make things right with Wendy when I get home. But tonight, Jesus, it's about You and not me." By the time I get home, I cannot even remember what we were arguing about.

The enemy loves to do anything he can to get condemnation flowing through your mind. When you feel condemnation, you are much less likely to pray. When you are at peace, it is easier to pray—and expect healing to happen. Put another way, if you cannot believe that you are clean in God's eyes, you simply will not enjoy the benefits. It is harder to let grace flow through you when your mind is clogged with what you are not.

I remember sitting in a pew one Sunday before I was able to grasp these things, thinking, *I dread dying the way a fat man dreads fasting.* I could not tolerate the idea of dying. I shook when I drove past a cemetery. I wish I were kidding, but I am not. The reason I dreaded dying was my false picture of God. Then I grabbed hold of the revelation that Jesus crashed onto the earth and had one big party declaring, "God is kind, and He sent Me to reconnect you to Himself."

I was in South Africa recently and met a young man who was struggling with his concept of God. I asked him to tell me about the kindest person he had ever met. He could not think of one single person in his entire life whom he would label "kind." This young man watched as our team prayed for quite a few people with physical problems. Two in particular stand out in my mind. They both had back problems and were very surprised to admit that after they were prayed for they felt a lot better. Our team prayed simple prayers and tried our best to explain how God is a loving and kind God.

I wanted so badly to reach out and hug this young man who was struggling. As we continued to talk, we landed on the idea that perhaps his view of God was distorted. I shared my story with him and we bonded in our commitment to attack anything in our thinking that misrepresents who God really is.

I think about Jesus as He walked with His Father on this earth, and it is intoxicating. I am not talking about Joseph, by the way. I am talking about the One who spoke from a cloud to His baby boy. I wish I had been there to hear that voice say, "This is my beloved Son, in whom I am well pleased" (Matthew 3:17, KJV). The very idea of God thinking the same thing about me seems heretical. But as I get older, it sounds less and less so.

I have seen dramatic healings over the years, but the ones that stand out in my mind are the ones in which it actually starts to click for people how kind the Father is and how much He honors and loves His children. Lazarus was raised from the dead, but he eventually died again. There is one healing, however, that continues from here into the next lifetime: freedom from condemnation.

Walking on this earth in complete peace with the One who made it is the highest level of spiritual maturity. This is especially true when you are aware of what your flesh is capable of. Living in peace with the Father and receiving love from Him helps us live holier by accident than we ever accomplished on purpose.

This is the journey that Papa's death sent me on. But I still had many miles to go before I found peace and freedom. I had to discover that God was not out to get me. To do that, I had to face my pain.

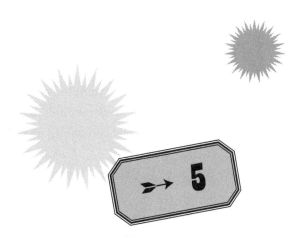

# Panic Attacks and Depression

It came from nowhere. One moment I was sitting on the edge of my bed thinking about whatever six-year-olds think about, and the next moment my heart was pounding, my head hurt, and my thoughts were racing all over the map. Irrational ideas from what seemed like hell itself came shooting at me: *What if I die tonight? What if I hurt myself? What if I choke in my sleep? What if I go crazy? What if I never leave this room again? What if this terror in my mind never goes away?*

If you have had a panic attack, you understand the depth of confusion and terror it brings. Plus, panic attacks seem to come and go at will. You never know when one is coming, and you never know when it will end. But it does end, and new anxiety about when the next one will strike takes over. *Tick, tock, tick, tock.* You watch the hands of your internal clock and think, *Dear God, please don't let this happen to me again. Please.*

It was not until I was in college that I stumbled across an infomercial about the Midwest Center for Stress and Anxiety and discovered that there was help for overcoming anxiety, depression and agoraphobia.

But that was many years away. This day I was six years old and too scared to tell anyone what had happened. All I knew was that it was a living hell. I was sure something terrible was wrong with me. I remember waking up one night unable to breathe, feeling as though someone had his hands clenched over my throat trying to kill me.

God said early in the game that it is not good for man to be alone, and panic attacks have shown me how true that is. People with panic disorder feel alone primarily because it is so hard to describe what is happening. If your arm is broken, you can show people your cast. If you have the flu, you have certain symptoms that can be diagnosed. But when it comes to panic disorder, you cannot get your hands around it. When I was growing up, there was no such thing as Google or WebMD. Back then most people had no idea what panic attacks were.

Sometimes I felt so disconnected from my body I just sat down and cried. I could look at something on TV, and my mind would spiral out of control. I began to talk about not feeling right, and my parents took me to the hospital. I can still see the nurse's unsmiling face as she took my blood pressure. I wanted to crawl inside of a hole and sit for ten eternities. I felt scared, hopeless, agitated, nervous and chaotic.

The attacks continued as I got older. I was driving to play basketball one night when, all of a sudden, I had to pull the car over because I was filled with terror. I did not know what to call it. I did not know whom to talk to. I did not know what to do.

When I turned eighteen, I could not take it anymore. I tried to explain to my parents how much I was hurting. As any good parent would, they sent me to my doctor, and he recommended medication. I went on Klonopin and Zoloft for depression and anxiety. Thus began a twelve-year journey of coping with panic through chemicals.

I hurt for people who have to take medication. I never judge anyone for it. At that point in my life, I could not see any other way out of the pain. The drugs calmed my mind but left me feeling lethargic. I slept a lot. I felt in many ways that I had lost who I was.

When I was in college, I kept the pill bottles on the shelf of my chest of drawers in my dorm room. Every time I took those pills, I thought, *I can't believe I am so weak that I have to take something to help me through the day.* My self-esteem took a nosedive. I felt that I had to explain my struggles and inferiority to others around me. The truth was that people had their own issues to deal with, and generally did not care that I was on medication. For me, however, it was the biggest deal in the world.

Shame invaded my life, and as the shame increased, so did the clinical depression. It is like a huge black cloud that follows your thoughts 24 hours a day. Even when you sleep you dream about it. It is as though you can never escape the spiral of negativity that grips your soul.

When I pray for people with clinical depression, I often get very emotional about their pain because I remember what that was like. I pray that as long as I live Jesus gives me opportunities to help people get set free. I hurt for people who are silently struggling with their own personal hells and think there is no way out. One day, I told my mom as we were walking into my doctor's office, "God will use this to help people one day." Now as I travel and speak about my story, men and women come up to me and say, "Thank God there is someone who struggles with the same thing, who understands."

My battle with panic disorder began to ebb and flow. There were some good seasons and some not so good seasons. Just when I thought I had whipped it, it reared its head. Even as I was writing this book and reflecting on my past, I had a three-week stretch when I battled anxiety. You would think that someone who is writing a book on the supernatural would just "suck it up and trust God," but that has not been my experience at all. It is possible to struggle with the messiness of life and see the supernatural at the same time.

We all have our battles; this was mine. But in the midst of these tough days, I started to get glimpses that I was not alone. I also began to experience strange things.

## Woe Is Me

In the summer of 1996, I was preaching at a summer-long sports camp, and a friend of mine handed me a book on the Holy Spirit. I was highly skeptical of the book and read it mainly to be able to dismantle it. Instead, it dismantled me. It created such hunger inside me for Jesus Christ that I did not know what to do. In a dorm room in Campbellsville, Kentucky, I said out loud, "I don't want to talk about Him this summer. I don't want to preach about Him. I want Him to walk through that door right there."

For three days, my spirit was fully alive, and I could not stop thinking about the Lord. One night that week, my team was watching the movie *Dead Man Walking*. Toward the end of the movie, I heard an audible voice in my right ear say, *Go to your room*.

I got up and started toward my room. As I made my way across the campus I could tell something unusual was about to happen. It was as though someone was walking with me. It is hard to explain. I had a sense that I should brace myself.

When I got into my room, I fell on the floor as though I weighed a ton and started weeping. The power and presence of God was so thick that I honestly thought I was going to die. I have never been more overwhelmed in my life. This was not a "time of reflection" where I contemplated the Lord. I wept and felt completely overwhelmed. I think it must have been the way Isaiah felt when he experienced the raw power and glory of God. After a while, a friend came looking for me, and as soon as he walked into the room he collapsed onto the floor and started weeping, too.

Even in the middle of the experience, I could not believe how intense it was. I would even use the word *terrifying* to explain it. Yet I was not afraid. How can something be terrifying but not make me afraid? I cannot say. Jesus' presence was consuming beyond my ability to describe it. Even three days after that experience I was exhausted from it. My sides were sore from crying and my eyes puffy. It was intense to say the least.

That encounter with the power of God fueled me to preach. He became real to me that night, and I knew in some way I would never again preach without a fire in my belly. Even though I still struggled with panic disorder from time to time, that encounter transformed my ministry. I found as well that I grew more and more comfortable talking about the disorder—especially when I discovered how many people struggled with the same thing.

I think many of us feel disqualified to experience God in out-of-the-box ways because we are aware of our own inadequacies, and we believe that they will keep us from experiencing Him. For me, when I read the Bible, I am encouraged because the people He interacted with had struggles as well.

Depression and panic attacks did not seem to keep Jesus at a distance in my life. He actually seems to be drawn to brokenness. I cringe when I hear of people being wounded by "faith" preachers who condemn others for any shortcomings in their journeys with Jesus. That is not the Jesus I have gotten to know.

## Plans Take Shape—Sort Of

After one summer of preaching, God told me clearly that I was supposed to go to Beeson Divinity School in Birmingham, Alabama, on the campus of Samford University. That idea had to be from God, because I never in a million years wanted to attend seminary. My dad told his friends that I was planning to go to "The Seminary," which made me laugh. He still seems to think that there is one seminary in the world where all the preachers get herded like sheep.

Seminary was also a stretch for me because of my college experience. Like many college students, I was lazy with my study habits. I put most of my focus on watching a very average football team at the University of Georgia. Most of us growing up in Georgia were raised to be Georgia Bulldogs. "Bulldog born, Bulldog bred, and when we die, we'll be Bulldog dead." I was brainwashed at an early age about the Bulldogs, and I am now passing that on to my children.

My grades stank. I had an incredible roommate named Chris "Block" Lynch who specialized in cooking. Instead of studying, I ate my way to a 1.9 GPA. I dated Papa John's for a couple of years before God intervened and brought a bombshell named Wendy across my path.

She was not interested in me. I cannot blame her. At that time I was in a stage of wearing sweatpants, orange boots, and the same hoodie sweatshirt every day. I was her "safe" fat friend who hung out with her after she went on dates with other guys. I was a sensitive listener, and I loved Jesus. We could wind up laughing and crying all in one setting. Little did I know that that would prove to be the secret for hitting the jackpot for life. It was genius.

I see young guys all the time trying to impress their potential lady friends by acting as though they have everything together. Recently I had a conversation with a friend I will call Stan. It went like this: "Stan, you are going about it all wrong. Instead of trying to impress her with how great you are, let her see you be tender. Allow her to know that you are not a Spirit-filled John Wayne."

Stan knew that he could not ignore what I was saying. If you saw me with my wife, you would wonder what my secret is, too. Stan said to me, "I don't know how to do that."

I responded, "Then you will stay single until Jesus Christ comes back to earth."

I am not sure if Stan got the message, but I did, because my only hope with Wendy was to be genuine.

With all of that going on, I barely graduated. I am still not sure how it happened. For years, I had dreams of UGA contacting me and saying, "We made a mistake. You still have one calculus class to go." Still, when God told me to go to Beeson, I thought, *Okay, I'll start in January*. I never considered the possibility that I might be rejected by a divinity school. I could expect getting rejected from medical school or law school or business school, but not seminary. It is a bad day when you are not allowed to study God.

The funny thing is, I was feeling good before the bad news came. I had bought a treadmill from K-Mart and lost a bunch of weight, kicked Papa John's to the curb, and asked Miss University of Georgia to marry me. She said yes, and I put a diamond on her finger. We were about to set sail on our own little Billy Graham movie.

But then my ship sank. I remember well the letter from the admissions director at Beeson. It was addressed to "William," which is my first name. It is never good when someone calls me "William." The letter said, "Dear William, your grades stank at Georgia, and God hates you, so our answer is no." These were not the exact words, but that is what it sounded like to me. My parents had already bought a cake and balloons to celebrate. This was not a good situation. After I read the letter, I walked to my room, got on my knees and told God, "You called me to go to Beeson. I don't know what to do. It's Your problem, not mine."

I could not articulate it then, but I somehow trusted that this rejection was not my problem. After all, I did not call myself to seminary. God did. So in my mind, it was His responsibility and not my burden to carry.

## That Was Quick!

During that time, my parents bought a house from a pastor named Benny who was moving to Birmingham to pastor a church there. Not long after I prayed about getting rejected from God's school, our phone rang. It was Benny. He introduced himself and asked if he could speak to my parents.

Before I passed the phone along, I asked him if he had any connections at Beeson since he was now a pastor in Birmingham. Benny said that, as a matter of fact, he was just about to have lunch with the dean. When I heard this, I said, "Beeson told me that I can't go to school there. Is there any way you could put in a good word for me?"

Within about a day, Beeson's admission's director called me and said, "The dean would like to give you a chance to prove yourself. Welcome to the Beeson family." So one bright morning my dog, Millie, and I took off on I-85 South pulling a U-Haul. Two professors, Dr. Robert Smith Jr. and Dr. Calvin Miller, were waiting for me. I had never heard of either one of them, and they sure had never heard of me. Yet by God's design, these two men would redirect the course of my life. I know it sounds a little dramatic to say it like that, but that is exactly what happened.

I married Wendy in 1997, and we settled into seminary life. Some friends from our church were in the same apartment complex. We called it our own little Melrose Place. God opened the door for me to pastor college students at The

Church at Brook Hills in Birmingham. I had a good rhythm of school and work for a few years as I helped Christian students work through their college obsession with Calvinism. I like John Calvin. I even hacked my way through his *Institutes of the Christian Religion* while I was in seminary. But sometimes I feel as though I need a vacation after a conversation with a passionate Calvinist. I was given a grace to help students exhale as they hammered out their own theology.

While I was at Beeson, a mentor asked me if I had ever considered having counseling. I did consider it, and it was one of the best decisions I would ever make.

## "Excuse Me, God, But I Hate You"

Let me state this bluntly: Until eight or nine years ago, I hated God. I never had a problem with Jesus, but I thought His Father was the epitome of meanness. It took counseling to lead me to this revelation. Can you imagine how shocked I was? I was working toward my master's in divinity and I hated God.

The road I walked backward to get to the point where I started to hate God included eye-opening counseling sessions and long conversations with my wife and friends. That era seems foreign now because all I do is minister the love of the Father as I pray for the sick, broken and hurting. But it was not foreign then.

Today, at this point in my life as a middle-aged pastor, I am slow to trust anyone who has not been through some form of counseling. That is because my counselors served as consultants to my soul. They pointed out things in me that

I had never thought about before. Counseling was so helpful for me that I wondered how I made it so long without it. But that is not to say it was easy. I am sure there were many times my wife thought, *God, why did You lead me to this man?*

I meet people all the time who want to have positions of godly authority like Moses, yet very few of us want to go to the backside of the desert. Many of us would like to have the impact Paul did, but who wants to be shipwrecked, stoned, bitten by a snake and persecuted by the religious establishment? Joseph has a great story, but who in the world wants to go through thirteen years in a pit or in slavery or in prison?

Yet you will be hard-pressed to find anyone in the Bible who made a great impact for the Kingdom without going through the wringer. To be great at what the Father has called you to be great at, you have to know who you are; difficult times and good counselors reveal that.

Jesus went into the desert, and I have a hard time believing that He loved every second of it. I generally want to backhand the person who came up with the proverb, "Our biggest breakdowns lead to our biggest breakthroughs." But that person is right. That truth hurts. Even in seasons when it looks as though Satan is winning his war against us, the Father has a way of turning those seasons into beauty.

## Love Steps In

When I was about six years old, I loved hanging out with a girl named Michelle. She had a sister named Sherry, and we played all day in my grandmother's backyard. I remember making up games like Dragon Champion, in which I defended my two friends from a killer dragon. My inner manly desire to conquer the bad guy was coming out.

I secretly wanted to kiss Michelle on her mouth but was too afraid to bring it up. I figured that if I could kill enough dragons, Michelle would throw her arms around me, look into my eyes and say, "You are the man of my dreams and I thank God He has given you to me. Kiss me, you animal." But it never went down that way.

One day Michelle made me mad. Since my inner manliness was not getting her attention, I chose a different tactic. I picked up a rock from the driveway and slung it at Michelle's head. I have always had good hand-eye coordination; I am a ping-pong kind of guy. That day I was accurate, and the rock hit Michelle smack on the forehead.

The following ten minutes looked like a crime scene. Michelle sat on the driveway bleeding and screaming. Adults came running from every direction like a cattle stampede. Remorseful, I muttered my first cuss word under my breath.

I remember Mr. Charlie yelling at me, "Chad, what did you do?" Sherry piped up: "Chad hit Michelle with a rock!" I felt as though I had sinned against all of heaven. I did not know what to do. I just stood there and soaked up every bit of condemnation I could. Then my grandmother told me to go to my room.

If you are a kid, is there any worse punishment than being sent to your room? Every second in there feels like an eternity. It is misery at its finest. I now relish every opportunity to send my children to their rooms. I think it is a reflex from the times I was sent to mine.

In my room that day, I braced myself for the worst. I figured that my grandmother was going to send me home to my parents, who would ship me off to boarding school and then straight into the military. At six this is a pretty terrifying life plan.

Mama Jane walked into that room and she was crying. I thought, *Dear God, if I die in a few minutes, I'm sorry for all of the stupid stuff I have ever done.*

I hold my grandmother in the highest regard of anyone I have ever met, and one reason is her tenderness. The way she looked at me that day showed me a glimpse of Jesus. She said that she was not happy with me, yet she loved me. She loved me so much that she was actually crying out of compassion for me. This was not a blithe "I love you" someone says while walking out the door. She looked into my soul.

Mama Jane said to me, "Chad, what you have done today is very, very bad. You should never throw a rock at anyone when you are mad. Why did you feel the need to throw that rock?"

I was now crying, too. I said, "Nobody loves me. They didn't want to play with me anymore."

My grandmother held me and said, "Chad, I love you very much. I'll always love you." She stepped into my mess and cleaned it up. She loved me even when I was down. She also brought reconciliation between Michelle and me that day. Lesson learned, we played amiably again.

It is fascinating to me how an incident that happened so many years ago can still remind me of the kindness of God. Most of us have built-in meters that register how mad He is on any given occasion and affirm that He stands ready to give us what we deserve. As a forty-year-old normal guy who is still trying to discover what God is like, I am continually amazed to find that He truly is forgiving, loving, compassionate, tender and kind.

I honestly do not know where I would be without the influence of my grandmother. Some people can give us glimpses of a God who loves to step into the middle of our chaos and pain and bring peace to it. Those who have the ability to do this are few and far between. Most people are fighting and clawing for their own promotions. But every once in a while, you meet someone who seems to be interested in your wholeness as much as you are.

If you ever find this kind of person, learn all you can. He or she probably learned that trait from the King, who turns even the worst things into the best. I can attest to this because that is precisely what God has done for me—even though in my pain and depression, I hated Him. It would not be long before I realized I was very wrong.

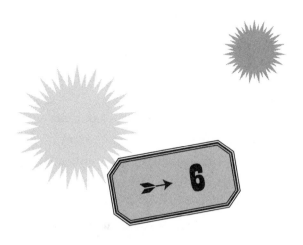

# "I'm Your Healer;
# Trust Me"

As my seminary studies came to a close, my wife and I, along with two close friends, Dave and Kim, heard God calling the four of us to move to my hometown of Spartanburg, South Carolina, and start a ministry to young adults called Wayfarer.

Dave and I had read a book called *Notes from a Wayfarer* written by Helmut Thielicke, a German theologian. The story of this man's life was greatly inspiring and had a powerful impact on the two of us as young leaders. Our hero in seminary was Dr. Robert Smith Jr., and he introduced us to Thielicke at a pivotal point in our story together.

In the meantime, I had told God that I would move anywhere in the world to do His ministry—anywhere but

Spartanburg. I used to tell my wife that I would move to a port-a-potty, but I was not going back home. I wanted to stretch my wings and live in a place where I would not be known to so many people as Little Chad.

But God is God, and I am not. So we packed our bags and took off. Through Wayfarer, we focused on preaching, teaching and writing curriculum to help young adults want to follow Jesus Christ with all of their hearts. We did this by coming alongside churches and providing them with resources that could help their congregations grow in Jesus. We also traveled quite a bit speaking at camps, conferences and different churches.

Our weekly worship service, called Engage, proved to be a valuable asset for many young people. Dave and I cut our teeth as we learned to minister to those in the midst of the difficult twenty-something life phase. Wayfarer put on Engage for young adults from all over upstate South Carolina. We watched as Jesus used the services as a catalyst to help these individuals figure out how to follow Him. Even now, about once a month, I run into someone who was deeply affected by Engage.

During this era of my life, I decided that, since I was getting older and Wendy and I were expecting our first child, I should come off of all medication for anxiety and depression. I loved ministering to people and sharing the message of God with them, and, honestly, I was no longer in counseling and was weary of being on medication. It seemed to be a great idea—but my follow-through was all wrong. I learned the hard way that life has a way of getting bumpy when you take matters into your own hands.

## A Huge Mistake

Some medications have powerful effects on the body, and that generally includes medications for anxiety and depression. I decided to stop taking the Zoloft and Klonopin, but I (foolishly) did not check with my doctor. I had no idea that you pay a big price for coming off of medications like those cold turkey. I tapered off way too fast after being on those medications for twelve years.

Today there are organizations like Point of Return in Westlake Village, California, that help people come off of medications without sending their central nervous systems into shock. I know that now, and I wish I had known that then. My body rebelled, hard. My head hurt so badly I did not want to open my eyes. I had a burning sensation and tingling in my brain. I felt foggy, and my neck hurt. Some days seemed like an eternity.

Things got so bad that I began to journal. I am not proud to admit that I hate journaling. I want to be a good "journaler." I wish I could be cool and head to Starbucks with a leather journal, a fancy pen, skinny jeans and a $30 coffee mug. But I have none of those things. If I tried to put on a pair of Diesels, I would throw my back out. Yet in this season of pain, I was journaling more than Henri Nouwen. Many times, the only thing I could do to get through the day was to write down my thoughts.

Have you ever been there? Have you ever had something happen to you that makes the clock seem stuck? I remember staring at the clock many days wishing night would hurry up and come so that I could get into bed and lie there. I cannot tell you how many sleepless nights I endured. And when I did sleep, I had dreams of me in my casket, people trying to kill me and storms coming at me. I kept functioning and ministering, but the days were long and hard.

## Darkness Falls

My problems were not just physical and emotional. True, I was battling sickness from chemical detoxification, but I was also going through a season of spiritual warfare. You might wonder how I could make a distinction between withdrawal and warfare, considering the wrenching bodily effects of going off certain medications. I can only say that I was learning more about the spiritual realm, and that included the enemy's attacks.

Among other nightmares, I could sense that our house had a dark presence in it. I walked around praying and anointing doorposts, pictures, TVs and our furniture with oil, committing our lives to the Lord again and again. If you come to our house today, you will find a picture on which you can still see where I put a heavy dose of oil.

I figured that I would just "tough out" the cold turkey withdrawal, since I had come this far, but the spiritual battle seemed to have no answers. I did not know of a single church that I could go to for help. Can you imagine walking up to a pastor and saying, "Pastor, a presence of evil is living in our house. Could you come take a look?" Me, either.

But then something happened for Wendy and me that changed everything. In a random encounter at an event at which I was speaking, I met a woman who gave me her dad's business card. He was a counselor in Titusville, Florida, and he understood spiritual attacks. So Wendy and I drove nine hours to seek Roger's help. Desperation, as I said earlier, does not seem to move God, but it sure will move a person. And when you move quickly toward Him, you seem to find Him more quickly.

## Meeting My Healer

When we arrived at Roger's office, I was on the edge of sliding out of touch with reality. I had loved Jesus most of my life, but I could not explain why I was going through what I was going through. I was scared.

Spiritual warfare and the physical symptoms of withdrawal were overcoming me. I kept thinking, *How pathetic is it that I have to drive all of this way to meet with someone because I can't figure out what is going on with me?* I had had some rough spots with Jesus but this was one of the toughest.

Roger welcomed my wife (who was now eight months pregnant) and me into his office. He then explained that he was going to invite the Holy Spirit to help us during the next three hours. I know: novel concept. We prayed through various things in my past that I had told him about, and then it happened. Roger was leading me in a prayer, when out of nowhere Jesus walked up to me in a vision and said, *I'm your Healer; trust Me.*

This was not an impression or a mental image; I was *seeing* Him. I had never heard of anything like this before. Jesus was about 5-foot-11 and 180 pounds. He had light brown hair, a light beard and wore a white tunic. Angels stood on either side of Him. One of them had a huge sword, and the other did not.

From the time I was a child I had heard stories about this man named Jesus. I went to Vacation Bible School as a little boy and listened to the teachers' descriptions of Him. My grandmother would talk about Him, and to Him, and tell me dramatic scenes from the New Testament. My little mind was filled with wonder: *I wish I could walk on water,* I thought. He fascinated me all of my life.

And here I was looking at Him. As He looked at me, His eyes pierced through me with violent gentleness. It was over-powering. It is a waste of time to try to describe what His love was like. I simply cannot.

But what I am telling you is true: I saw Jesus that day. If you want to chuck this book into the trash, I understand. I have always been skeptical when people write about things like this. Yet, it happened.

What separated this experience from the one I had had a few years earlier in my dorm room in Campbellsville was that in Campbellsville I did not see anything. In that instance, I was overwhelmed by the glory of almighty God. But this time, it was like watching a movie—except it was more real than that. I was *in* the movie. I honestly have no idea what to call it. Some use the term *open vision.* The one thing I know is that everything changed for me in that moment.

And it was not only that I saw Him: Jesus came to me and held me close. I have never felt love like that in my life. I hit the floor. My wife, alarmed, asked, "What happened?" It was a while before I could speak.

If at this point you think I was crazy, I understand. I thought I was crazy, too. But it happened. I have been reluctant to talk about that day too much because I thought that people would find it hard to believe. I never want to come across as an idiot. So I decided it was best to keep my mouth shut about the encounter. I was not at a worship service. I was not caught up in some glory cloud. I was a conservative type of guy with a health problem. I was a Baptist to the core who secretly never wanted to walk out on the waters of anything that would draw attention.

Yet in that one moment, everything changed for me. I cannot tell you how many times I prayed to Jesus: "Wreck me with who You are. I want all of You. Show me who You are." I know I never expected Jesus to answer those prayers of mine like that. Yet Jesus Christ of Nazareth walked up to me in an open vision. That was way out of my comprehension. I had no paradigm for it.

I wonder how our biblical heroes felt when weird stuff happened to them. Can you imagine being Cornelius and having an angel walk up to you and say, "Hey, how's it going? God likes you and your offerings" (see Acts 10:1–6).

Thomas did not have a vision of Jesus; the resurrected Jesus came strolling in as though He was looking for something to eat and said, "Thomas, go ahead and touch My hands and My side" (see John 20:27). The Bible offers an extensive list of people who had interactions with God. We love to talk about those people, but we often have a hard time comprehending it when it happens to us.

We seem to listen more carefully to pastors and leaders who are really smart and can give the dimensions of the boat Noah built. I understand that. People have fabricated stories of signs and wonders over the years, abusing what some call charismatic things. But we cannot use that as an excuse to hide behind a false pretense of who Jesus is and what Jesus is like.

People who fight against "experiences" with God so furiously generally fear experiencing Him. It is possible to memorize the book of Galatians and not know the God of the Bible. Rather than consider those encounters as "weird," it should be weirder to follow a supernatural God and never experience the supernatural. If my life is not super*natural* to some degree, then it is super*ficial* to a great degree.

I have heard many times, "Don't be so heavenly minded that you are no earthly good." It might be truer that we are so earthly minded that heaven has a hard time doing much good through us. I have been asking the Lord to get me to a place in my life where I can live consistently with one ear there and one here. In Roger's office that day, I discovered that that is the only way I want to live.

## Diving into Love

When I saw the Lord, His love knocked me out of my chair. It was not a handshake love. It was a messy, wild, passionate, deep, perfect love. It was the kind of love that makes you not care what anyone else in the world thinks about you. Because of that experience, I can see why the early Christians laughed as Nero burned them at the stake. They had such revelation of the love of God that they did not care even about death. When I say I felt love, it is an understatement. All I could say to Wendy, when I could speak, was, "He is so full of love."

Ten years later I can still picture Him the way He looked that day. As I mentioned, I have told this story only rarely.

One time I tried to tell about it at a conference. The conference was great, people were connecting with me, and Jesus was doing some wonderful ministry. But when I shared this story—*bam!* It was like hitting a brick wall. My encounter with Jesus went over like a pregnant pole vaulter—that is to say, not well.

A few weeks ago, I was talking about these events from the stage of our church, including the warfare details, and a man got up and took his three kids out of the service. He will probably never come back to our church.

Maybe part of the reason that stories like this are hard to comprehend is that so many individuals have been manipulated in the name of Jesus. Perhaps it is also because people know Jesus from a historical standpoint rather than as a present-tense Savior.

The early disciples did a lot of ministry in the supernatural, and they did not even have a New Testament. We have ten Bibles in every house, and yet we get nervous when unusual things happen—even when those things parallel the stories we find in those Bibles. Instead, we should recognize when Jesus shows up in our lives in supernatural ways. After all, He did say, "My sheep listen to my voice" (John 10:27).

A couple of nights after my encounter with Jesus Christ, I told Him out loud as I sat on my futon, "Show me everything. I want to know You. I want to know You and God the Father so well that I don't know where I begin and where You end. I want intimacy with You. I want such deep friendship with You that I smell like You. I'm Yours." I told the Holy Spirit that I surrendered to Him and His power to the best of my ability.

When you get to the point in your life that you are tired of flirting with Jesus and the Kingdom and you are ready to give yourself to Him, He will see to it that you have a catalyst moment. After that vision, I was "all in." Looking back on my last ten years, I can say that this process has been gentler and calmer than I was expecting. Perhaps you do not have to be obnoxious to walk in the ways of heaven after all. I still think about how natural Jesus was when I saw Him. He simply told me that He loved me.

## Getting to Know Him

It was after this experience that I decided to do something I had never done before—really read the gospels.

I had learned at Beeson that the first chapter of Hebrews paints a picture of Jesus and His Father as being identical. If that was true, and I believed it to be, then something was wrong with my view. I had never felt love such as I felt with Jesus, and, according to the Word, that is the way His Dad is, too. I think this is what Paul talked about in Ephesians 3:14–21 when he said that he prayed for us to be filled with the full measure of God's love and then described that love. I wanted to know more.

Thus, I did not jump into the gospel kiddie pool with inflatable water wings. I cannonballed into the deep end Rambo-style and swam as if my life depended upon it. I score as an ENFP on the Myers-Briggs Type Indicator, which translates into "Let's *go* for it." That is the way I operated in this instance. I wanted to know just how much I could trust Jesus Christ and expect to see His Kingdom power at work.

For a long season, I had my head buried in the gospels so intently that I ignored my usual hobbies. I will never forget the night Wendy said, "I just wish you would watch *SportsCenter* for a change." I never thought in a million years I would hear her say that. But as I started observing Jesus in the gospels, His Father opened my eyes to realities I had never known. The longer I stayed in the gospels, the more my grid of what it means to follow Jesus began to change.

Have you ever noticed that people who walk in what is perceived as "extreme faith" make those around them either incredibly tense or incredibly inspired? There seems to be no neutral ground. The more time you observe the way Jesus operated in the natural realm, the more it will affect the way in which you go about your daily life.

## Desperate Desire

When I was in seminary, Dr. Smith told me a story about a twelve-year-old boy who wanted to know God. It has been a while since I heard it but I remember it this way. This young fellow was so intent on his quest that he went from hut to hut in his African village trying to find someone who could help him find God. After knocking on doors one day, he met a man who said, "I can't help you, but I know someone who can. Up that path is a sage who lives up in the hills. He can help you."

The young boy immediately started the long journey up that path. After walking uphill for hours, he came to the sage's hut and knocked on the door. He was exhausted from his walk but desperate to find the answer to his question on how to find God. The door opened slowly, and a short old man with a long beard walked out. The man looked to be a hundred years old, but the boy was undeterred.

He blurted out, "I want to know God."

The old man stared at him in silence and then motioned for the young fellow to follow him.

The boy followed the sage to a pond. Still silent, the old man motioned for the boy to look closely into the water. As soon as the youngster's head was bent down, the sage grabbed the back of his neck and pushed his head under the water.

The boy started kicking and shaking in an effort to loose himself from the grip of the sage. He feared that he had walked all that way just to be killed by some old lunatic! Just as the boy was losing strength, the sage pulled him out of the water. They sat at the water's edge for a couple of minutes, the youth staring at the sage, still gasping for breath.

The sage broke his silence and said sternly, "When you want God as much as you just wanted your next breath," he said, "you will find Him."

God did not change for me over the three years of this season; I changed. I stayed so single-minded about learning to trust Him that nothing else—not even my next breath—mattered. I could not get into the Word enough. I spent more time in prayer during that time than I had in the previous five years. I went after the King and the Kingdom as hard as I could.

My desperate desire led me to the gospels, and the gospels lead me to Jesus. Jesus led me to the Father, and that is where I have been ever since. When you find the Father, you find everything.

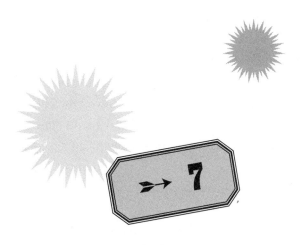

# Elliptical Madness

As I mentioned before, I have a track record for making impulsive purchases. Last Christmas I got a report from my doctor that my blood pressure was high and that I needed to lose some weight and quit eating so badly. So I did what any man with a task before him would do: I headed to the sporting goods store. The store happened to be running a special on elliptical machines. I begged Wendy to let me buy one.

She was reluctant, and her reluctance was not unfounded. I cannot tell you how many times I have decided to improve my health. One time in seminary, I thought about buying something I saw on an infomercial that would make my gut go away. With that product, you could do sit-ups without doing sit-ups. But my wife stared at me and said, "We will not be ordering anything to shock your abs."

Still, she finally agreed that this elliptical machine was a good idea. When I say machine, I want you to think of a contraption that is bigger than a Ford Focus. At the time, we were living in a small rental house. When the men came to deliver this beast, Wendy could not believe how big it was. She asked me where it was going, and I said confidently that it was going in our bedroom. It dwarfed the room. It looked ridiculous and extreme. But six months later, my blood pressure was back to normal thanks in large part to that elliptical machine.

Sometimes you have to be extreme. But it is also possible that what some call extreme, the Father may call a normal day in pursuing Him.

## Which Way Is Up?

In seminary I had a mentor who used to tell me, "Get your theology from the Bible. Don't take your theology to the Bible and interpret it through your own paradigms." It is not unusual to read the latest Christian bestsellers and then interpret the Bible through those books. The most exciting thing I have ever done spiritually is read the gospels and let Jesus tell me what my reality is.

For many years all I preached about was being born again and going to heaven when you die. If I preached it once, I preached it a thousand times. I had evidently gotten over my kitchen-table angst. But there is a small hitch. Jesus never publicly preached the message of being "born again." He did tell Nicodemus in a one-on-one conversation that being born again was a big deal (see John 3). Why is it a big deal? According to Jesus, the Kingdom of God was a reality on earth—not just heaven—and you had to be born again to operate in it.

Nicodemus, like a lot of people, had difficulty with this. He knew that God was with Jesus because of the works He did, but he stumbled over the revelation about the Kingdom of heaven coming to earth—the idea of experiencing the Kingdom in the here and now.

Jesus explained further that He would be "lifted up" so that we can look upon Him and have eternal life—the way that Israelites who were bitten by poisonous snakes were restored to life if they looked up at the bronze serpent on the pole. Eternal life is not just an idea of going somewhere when you die; it is the reality of becoming whole while you live. The Greek word for *life*, *zoe*, means "abundant life; fullness of life."

Can you imagine what it must have been like from Satan's perspective after Jesus was resurrected? The earth now had lots of people doing the same works that Jesus had done. That is why Satan attacked the early Church so viciously, and used his craftiness to lure her away from the mission Jesus gave her. Satan realized early on that he could not defeat the Church—but he *could* influence people to misrepresent this message about the Kingdom residing here on earth. He works to get the message about Jesus Christ so off track that we have no idea which way is up anymore.

Jesus said, "Do not believe me unless I do the works of my Father" (John 10:37). Do you know what this means? It means that Jesus expects the works to continue through us. This is why He said, "It's better for you if I go, for then the Holy Spirit can come" (see John 16:7). When I realized this, as I have mentioned, it changed the focus of my preaching away from going to the right place when you die. Eternal life is not just off in the great by and by. It is now. It is deep, abundant intimacy with the One who offers even better wholeness than Moses offered in that desert. It is intimacy that not even death can end.

In John 17:3, Jesus gives us a complete commentary of what eternal life is. He says: "Now this is eternal life, that they may know you." He is praying to His Father in that passage. It is hard to fathom what would happen to the Church if we had true revelation of what Jesus is saying here.

Eternal life is a real, deep connection with the God of the universe. It is, further, the understanding that He is not only God, but also our *Father*. The journey to this place of understanding is one that costs us everything. Yet in this invitation to know Him deeply, we find what we are looking for.

For most of my life I lived Bono's lyrics: "I still haven't found what I'm looking for." I knew I was missing something, I just did not know what it was. Jesus shows us in John 17:3 what we are missing. Walking naturally in the supernatural is not about reading charismatic books and memorizing verses about the Kingdom. It is about one thing: Eternal Life. As we get to know our Father in the way that Jesus talked about, the supernatural becomes more normal. It is not about chasing the supernatural; it is about chasing the One who holds the supernatural in His hands.

One day, Jesus' disciples asked their Rabbi how to pray. He basically said, "Pray like this: 'Our Father in heaven, great is Your name. May Your Kingdom come to the earth as it is in heaven.'" (You can find the exact quote in Matthew 6:9–13.) Our Father loves to reward those who go after Him (see Hebrews 11:6). He loves faith, and the reason that so many of us do not exercise our faith more is that we feel like failures most of the time. I know I do. Yet look at the ones Jesus taught how to pray: It was messy people—the disciples.

The Father loves to use messy people to activate the power of the Kingdom on earth. Messy people need to know they are loved. And when they believe they are, faith is the natural expression of that intimate love. Personally, I think we have very few faith problems and very many love problems.

## Treasure Hunting

I have no idea who came up with the term *Treasure Hunting* to describe listening to the Holy Spirit and doing whatever He says, but I love it. Recently, Oliver, pastor of students at our church, suggested the youth group do some treasure hunting. He invited me to join in.

I sat down at a table with four teenagers and my son Sam, who was eight years old at the time. Someone pulled out a piece of paper, ready to write down our instructions, and we said, "Holy Spirit, where in the city do You want us to go? Whom do You want us to minister to?" We immediately heard, *Go to downtown Greenville.* We then agreed that we were supposed to pray for a man who was going to be walking his dog.

We headed out in my supernatural minivan and went straight to a park. As soon as we got there, we saw a man walking a big dog. I asked him if he needed prayer for anything. At first, he looked at me as if I had five noses. But we were very relaxed about it, and the Lord ministered to him by encouraging him with some prophetic words. After the fact, he commented on how great the experience was.

Rather than leave, we decided to hang around for a bit. Two minutes later a man sat down on a bench. We learned that his name was Kevin. Kevin was homeless, but you would never know it. He was well dressed and shaved.

I asked him if our guys could pray for him. He started crying, and then I witnessed something that made me cry. My son and a couple of the teenagers started to pour the love of heaven all over Kevin. It is one thing to pray a meaningful prayer over someone. It enters another realm to tell someone you have never met various things about his life and how much Abba loves him. I did not pray for Kevin. I sat back and watched these students from our church act like Jesus.

We ended up taking Kevin to a grocery store to buy him some necessities. A family at City Church bonded with Kevin and helped him get back on his feet. There is no substitute for being a person, family or church that is all about the Father's presence. A blank sheet of paper, a pen and the willingness to listen to the Holy Spirit helped two people in gentle and powerful ways.

At our church we enjoy talking about *purpose* and *methods*. We love strategy sessions. Likewise, I love leadership ideas. I have been obsessed with the book *Good to Great* by Jim Collins (HarperBusiness, 2001) for the past several months. Yet what trumps everything is the Father's presence. When you are driven by His presence, you see impossible things happen on a regular basis.

Let me give you another example. Recently, I had an appointment in a local coffee shop. I drink very little coffee, but it makes me feel cool to go in there. One small problem: I had my days mixed up and the person I was supposed to meet never arrived. As I was walking to my van to leave, the Father told me to go back. I immediately thought, *That's not God. That's my own mind.* I climbed into my van, but I could not shake the thought that I was supposed to go back.

I returned to the coffee shop, and saw a man sitting outside with a cigarette in one hand and a cigar in the other. That is pretty impressive. I asked him his name and he said Alex. I could tell that he was not in his right state of mind. I began to chat with him, and he told me that he was schizophrenic.

Alex had a cross around his neck, and I asked him about it. I had a hard time following his story, but when he finished I said, "Alex, can I pray for you?" He said that I could. I did not lay hands on him because I sensed I was not supposed to. I simply prayed that the Father would manifest His love to Alex. Alex's head slowly slumped over and his arms fell to his sides. He was there with me, but not "with me." I may never know what the Father showed him or said to him, but I know that Alex experienced the love of the Father that day. When he lifted his head, the look on his face was more peaceful. We talked a little more about life, and, honestly, God probably ministered more to me than Alex that day.

These stories point to one thing: "Normal" experiences with the Father change lives. Even if no notable differences take place in the people we are praying for, God has a tendency to show Himself to us when we push through our fears and step out in faith to show His love to others. These are not opportunities for us to walk into the spotlight; they are opportunities to help people connect to the real, alive Jesus and allow Him to do what He still loves to do.

When I wake up mornings I like to pray, "Holy Spirit, do something unusual through me today. Catch me off guard with how real You are." Six months ago I was in the kitchen making dinner for the family when I heard the Holy Spirit say, *Turn on the television.* I turned it on and clicked up a few channels. There was an African pastor named Surprise Sithole talking about the power of the Holy Spirit that he was seeing manifested in Africa. Sid Roth was interviewing Pastor Surprise here in America.

I was inspired by the childlike faith of this African man. I ordered his book, *Voice in the Night* (Chosen, 2012), and read it as soon as it came in the mail. Little did I know that I was being set up.

A few months after reading Pastor Surprise's book, I traveled to White River, South Africa, with City Church on a short-term mission project. When we arrived, our contact, Rich Hodge, said that the first thing we were going to do was travel to Michaels Children's Village, which is an Iris Ministries orphanage.

Rich said to me, "Pastor Surprise will be there."

I said, "Wait a minute. Who?"

When I figured out that this was the same man that the Holy Spirit had guided me to watch on TV, I started to laugh. I sincerely think that God loves to show us how real He and His Kingdom are.

Heaven is yearning for Christianity with demonstration. Deep theology with no experience is like a museum—big, beautiful and fun to explore, but at the end of the day it is just a building full of artifacts. I want more than that. I want a theology that leads me to believe that the dead can be raised and that atheists will come to Jesus.

The other day I joined some teenagers from City Church for another Treasure Hunt. We felt as though we were being led to go to Target, but we spent almost two hours there and did not have any sense of what we were to do. As a matter of fact we offered to pray for someone and were told no. We knew that we were supposed to pray for someone at Target, but, finally, we just left.

We drove to a nearby restaurant to see if anyone there needed prayer when I suddenly had the overwhelming desire to go to the other Target in our city. As soon as we pulled into that parking lot, I saw a young man sitting on a bench taking a break from working. He was an employee and his name was Mike. We said, "Hey, man, this is going to seem weird, but we think we are supposed to pray for you."

Over the next ten minutes we delivered a few words of knowledge for him, and he was touched with the love of God. We then went back to the church and raised money for him to help with a need he had. When he came to the church to pick up the money, many students prophesied over him and released the love of the Father into his heart. He was overwhelmed. I hugged him before he left, and I thought, *All of this because some teenagers decided to trust God and go into the city to do His works.*

Sounds like the book of Acts to me.

## Tell That Kid to Stop Running!

Recently at a conference that our church sponsored, we saw Jesus heal a woman with chronic back pain. Not only that, He literally removed the "hot pad" that she was using for relief. It just disappeared. She reached around to touch her back, which was now free from pain, and the pad was gone.

If that paragraph makes your eyes pop, I completely understand. If God had told me ten years ago that I would write about something like that, I would never have believed it.

If your heart is burning to see more of this, join the party. You do not need great faith. You need only revelation of the kind and gentle love that our Father has for His children. Then you need a little bit of courage to jump out there and go for it. This is not a challenge to you to leave your church and join the believers in your locale who experience these things. Just pray for people in your own church. Be gentle. Be unassuming. Be like Jesus. I have a suspicion that you will find that it has way more to do with love than with faith.

I clearly do not have all of the answers, but I am willing to go where He is sending me. And He is sending me into the land of the things that some have no desire to talk about. It is not a question of why certain things do and do not happen; it is a question of why so many believers resist the possibility of doing the things that His original disciples did.

In the past few years, in fact, our church has come under serious scrutiny and criticism by other disciples of Jesus Christ. Why? I think it is because humans are comfortable with things that are neat and tidy and manageable. Too many ministries around the country spend more time thinking about when the lights should go dim or bright in a service than they do praying for the drug addict on the third row or the woman with cancer on the fourth row. Surely Jesus died for more than well-organized church services.

Now don't get me wrong—if you come to our church, you will see that it is not a freak show. We plan our services. We maintain order. But we also love the idea of leaving room in our services for Jesus to work.

Still, we have borne the brunt of a lot of hurtful things these past few years. The big question from people is: "Why do you spend so much time focusing on healing and other things in the supernatural?"

My answer remains the same: "When I turned thirty years old, I became intolerant of my own preaching and experience with Jesus. I did not like the person I had become. I preached a fear-based Gospel message with practically no stories that looked like anything I see in the gospels and Acts. Then one night I prayed for a woman who was legally blind. God healed her, and I started to seek out what in the world I actually believed."

When I started walking on this road, I came to discover that He is full of love and that He desires to help broken people. Healings became less about a particular theology and more about a simple extension of His heart through my own broken self.

Think about that. Discipleship is something that everyone in every denomination believes in. We may have different views on what discipleship truly is, but at the end of the day, you will hardly ever find someone who believes in Jesus who will say that he or she is not a disciple.

This is how I wrestled with God on my own: *If Chad Norris considers himself a disciple of Jesus, then why in the world is he not doing what the disciples in the early Church did? Why are lame people not getting up in any service he is involved in? Why are the blind not seeing? Did Jesus all of a sudden have expectations of Chad Norris that are different from His expectations of His first disciples?*

I was not condemning myself for lack of experience. I did not look at it as I were some fungus in the eyes of God.

Actually, I felt like Curious George. I wanted to understand why I loved reading about Simon Peter so much but did not do the things he did. And why, if I were stranded on an island like Paul, would I consider it a fitting time to preach that sometimes God wants us to be miserable and alone? On the contrary, the Father healed everyone on the island through Paul's hands (see Acts 28:7–10).

Ever since I saw Jesus in the counselor's office that day, I became desperate to find the Father and live out His love in these extremely "normal" ways.

So I am simply asking, "Where have all the disciples gone?" The pressure gets taken off of me when I realize that I am not the healer. Of course, we know that none of us can heal a gnat. We simply pray and God blows our minds with how real He is.

Now, I sincerely believe that it is possible to be a sold-out disciple of Jesus Christ and never pray for one sick person. Some of the godliest people I know are not comfortable attempting the Father's works (see John 10:37). And on the other side of the coin, just because someone can pray for sick people and see them healed does not automatically mean that he is walking in purity and building great friendship with God.

As I was leaving church after a service one night, I saw a teenager racing around the sanctuary. I was going to go ask him to settle down and not disrupt those still receiving ministry. That was my plan until I learned that his torn Achilles tendon had been healed, and he was running because he was so excited.

That gives me hope. Instead of condemning ourselves or others for what we do or what we do not do, we can move into different cultures in our churches where messy people with their own issues can draw closer to the Father. I think that when that happens, we will start seeing as a matter of course what our Lord and His disciples saw while they were here. Is that extreme? Quite possibly it is extremely normal.

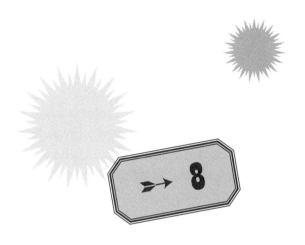

# Angels and Other
# Normal Things

I have led five teams on mission trips to Croix-des-Bouquets
in Haiti over the past year and a half. I still marvel at how
I found myself connected to this country.

One night a couple of years ago, I was in the Memphis
airport catching a connecting flight home from an event. I
was on the wrong side of the airport because I had walked
right past my gate. That was a first for me, but it proved to
be providential. That is where I ran into Chris.

I had first met Chris quite a few years before at an event
where I preached and he led the worship. After we chatted
and caught up for a few minutes, Chris asked if I would
pray for a friend of his named Gary Hypolitte who ministers
in Haiti. In one of the clearest examples in my life of the
Holy Spirit speaking to me, I heard a voice say, *Call Gary.*

Honestly, there are times when it is not even faith. When the Lord wants you to know that He wants something, you will hear Him.

I did not delay. I called Gary at the first opportunity. When he answered the phone and I told him who I was, he said, "An angel of the Lord told me that you would call me today." When certain people tell you that they heard from the Lord, you know they mean it. Gary is one of those people. I have never seen anyone walk with God the way Gary does. He tells story after story of God providing for his ministry in remarkable ways. Those things happen on a regular basis at Bethel Mission Outreach, his ministry in his native Haiti. Bethel has a school for three hundred children, a church and the only house of prayer in Haiti. The mission builds homes for families in the area, and Gary is in the process of building his first orphanage. (You can find more about the ministry at www.bethelmissionoutreach.org.)

When I stood in that hotel room many years ago and shook my Bible at the heavens, telling Jesus that I wanted to see the book of Acts in my life, one of the ways He answered was to cross my path with a Haitian who makes my walk with Him look pale and weak. I believe with all of my heart that if Jesus manifested Himself and walked through a locked door into a room where Gary was, Gary would say, "Hello, Lord, I love You." On the other hand, most of us would probably fall out of our earth suits. Just by being around this man, I am inspired to go after the Lord with intense passion.

The first time I walked onto Gary's property, I turned to a friend and said, "There are angels all over this place." I could somehow sense it. Unless you have ever been to Haiti, it is hard to understand the spiritual climate there. Spiritual warfare is not a topic of discussion at his compound; it is a reality.

Let me give you an example. He has an intercessory prayer team that prays every Monday through Friday from four to seven a.m. People from our church who have visited Bethel have said that taking part in that time of prayer was the most powerful spiritual experience of their lives.

One morning when Gary joined the early morning prayer team, one of the intercessors told him that she had dreamed the night before about someone trying to kill people on the property. Gary himself had dreamed that there was a battle in the heavenly realms about his ministry. That day at noon, several gunmen jumped the wall around the mission and started firing at the children and workers of Bethel.

Gary still does not know how he ended up in another room across the compound. He has no memory of how it happened. I believe that he was literally put there instantly by God. Let that sink in. The gunmen jumped back over the wall and took off. There were bullet holes everywhere, but no one was harmed.

Another time, voodoo leaders cursed Gary's property using skulls of dead animals. At a later time those same voodoo leaders were found dead in Croix-de-Bouquets. This sounds to me like something you would read about in Acts.

Haiti is one of the most beautiful and miserable places on the earth. When I think about paradox, I think of Haiti. Since the massive earthquake that occurred there in 2010, I cannot imagine a much worse place to live. Yet at the same time, I cannot think of a place more deeply spiritual and inspiring. Yes, voodoo is rampant in the country (its proponents boil water with their hands, for instance), but the message of Jesus is starting to rise all over this country.

I always enjoy watching the television show *Punk'd* because of the reactions of people who are placed in unusual situations and have to deal with them. I record that show and laugh out loud all the way through it. So you might imagine that taking a "religious" person to Haiti is as fun for me as going to the beach. My secret fantasy is to take every Bible scholar in America who thinks that the days of signs and wonders are over on a trip with me to Haiti. The Kingdom of God is in full effect there.

## Angels Make an Appearance

Let me tell you about an incident with Amos. He works for Gary at Bethel Mission Outreach.

All week long we had been preaching at a local church in Croix-des-Bouquets. Around four hundred people crowded into the tiny church every night, and Jesus showed up in power to heal the sick, cast out the enemy and lead lost people to Himself. It was fun, and the ministry times seemed very comfortable and natural. At one point we saw a group of children gather around a demon-possessed woman and pray heaven down on her. Nobody told the children to do this. They were expressing their experience of the presence of the Lord.

Amos walked up to me the final night of the revival and asked me to take his picture. I did not have a camera with me, but a team member did. She took a picture of him that soon had our team buzzing. In the background of the picture of Amos appeared several odd circles, various glowing orbs.

Now, on the plane ride to Haiti the Father had kept telling me, *I'm going to open your eyes to angels this week.*

Throughout the week we had sensed angelic activity in the room. I cannot explain why we thought this, because we never saw anything with our natural eyes. I can only say that we discerned the presence of something besides ourselves. After we saw Amos's picture, we took other pictures of the service. These pictures also revealed unusual shapes and colors around us.

The more we pondered this, the more we realized that God was allowing us to see spiritual realities—things apparently as real as the chair I am sitting on. As God did this, I noticed our response. We did not worship the angels. We did not talk to them. We did not bow down to them. Instead, we talked about how awesome God is. The presence of His ministering angels drew us more closely to the One who sits on the throne, the One the angels themselves worship.

On our next trip to Haiti, the same thing happened. We led a crusade and saw many, many Haitians come to hear the message of Jesus. Our team took pictures once again in which orbs appear in the background.

Similarly, I had a friend on the team pray over me before I preached one night, and he said that the Lord kept showing him a mental image of me covered by a blanket with different holes in it. Someone took a picture of me while I was preaching, and I could not believe what it showed: a huge blanket-looking thing with various holes in it. What was it? I have no idea. Yet, I cannot be talked out of how real heaven is and what an influence it has on our lives in the here and now.

I tell these stories to help you see that the Kingdom of heaven is present around us. Jesus is not simply the focus of endearing tales of long ago. He is the literal King of the universe. Heaven is real, and it is also closer than we think. On our last trip to Haiti, a voodoo parade marched right beside the stage where I was preaching. More than one hundred people who hated what we were doing marched in that parade. This caused some concern with our team. Can you imagine in your church this Sunday if a voodoo parade marched down the center aisle? We pressed in, prayed and preached the Kingdom. We had no other option. And nothing bad happened. There was no violence. Were we afraid? Of course. But we made the decision to trust God completely.

## A Matter of Awareness

We know that it is a bad idea to worship angels. I also think it is dangerous to talk about them too much. That is because, as normal as they are, they are not the point. The One who sends them is the point. At the same time, I think I would be stupid to ignore what God sends His angels to do.

When Jesus Christ was being arrested in the Garden, He said, "Do you think I cannot call on my Father, and he will at once put at my disposal more than twelve legions of angels?" (Matthew 26:53). Jesus was always aware of the unseen realm. The idea of angels was not strange to the One we give our lives to, so it should not be strange to us.

One night after preaching at a student camp in Texas a few years ago, I was asked to pray for the camp leadership. As I began to pray, the Holy Spirit led me to ask God to minister to the staff in the same way that He ministered to Jesus in the desert: with angels. For the next ten minutes some people were blown away by what happened and others were terrified. Some people on the team had glimpses of the angels. When you pray and think like a Kingdom citizen the natural realm tends to shift. When things like that manifest, you will find out very quickly if you have the maturity to steward them.

A few months before that notable trip regarding Amos's picture, I was asked to lead a weeklong Bible study for another church in our area. The week turned into several weeks, and before we knew it, we were seeing people set free in their thinking. Some of the people there had never seen prayer for healing, much less conducted in a calm and rational manner.

One of the men in that Bible study ended up going to Haiti with us. He told me that he will never be the same. I think that describes a lot of us. We had participants on that trip from many different churches (and different kinds of churches). Our common ground was that we all asked God to do whatever He wanted with and through us.

Once you see the Kingdom manifest with your own eyes, the game changes. But if you never get to the place where you ask to see these things happen—and mean it—then it will not be surprising if you go a lifetime without a single out-of-the-box encounter with God.

*Kingdom* is more than a popular buzzword. Paul says that "the kingdom of God is not a matter of talk but of power" (1 Corinthians 4:20). When the Father gave me revelation of this concept, I lost interest in preaching sermons that had no illustrations of His power attached to them. Too many sermons (including many that have come out of my own mouth) have valued eloquence over Holy Spirit power.

It is a matter of awareness. In Luke 18 we hear a blind beggar screaming, "Son of David, Son of David, help me!"

Jesus looked at that man and said, "Your faith has made you whole." That would get Jesus fired from many church staffs. Yet, the King said that, and we are left either to move on quickly or to embrace it.

Jesus will not force His works upon us; we have to want them. We call out to Him, believing that He wants to show us His grace. That blind beggar was not going to tolerate having Grace-in-the-Flesh walk past and leave him without a breakthrough. The people around him tried to get him to shut up but he simply would not. The Father loves to reward that kind of faith on the earth.

## Experiencing His Presence

Faith for the impossible is a normal state. When I have no faith for the impossible and no spiritual curiosity in my walk with Jesus, I need to ask myself some serious questions.

A few years ago, I was in College Station, Texas, with some friends who are part of a worship band. We were talking together late one night in one of our hotel rooms, and I wound up in a conversation with one of the men named Pat. He was about to head off to his room when I said, "Why don't we pray before you hit the rack?" I began with something like, "Father, we come into Your presence right now. . . ."

As soon as those words left my mouth, wind started blowing in the hotel room. Now, the air-conditioning unit was not running, but this wind came from the wall opposite the unit anyway. It was as though the aroma of heaven filled that hotel room. Our hands and feet felt freezing cold.

Pat started laughing and said, "Dude, are we about to be transported?" I replied that I had no idea. This went on for twenty minutes or so, and that was it. Why did our Father do that? What exactly did we experience? I cannot answer either question, but I know this: Curiosity about it is not a bad thing.

As I was starting to walk more in the Kingdom and see the supernatural manifest on a regular basis, I was also on the road a lot. One weekend I was leading a retreat for high school students with another worship leader and good friend named Matt. I will never forget taking exit 173 on I-85 South heading toward Lavonia, Georgia, for that event.

We held our service that night, and the Father ministered to many people. Matt and I went back to the house on Lake Hartwell where we were staying. We played some ping-pong, and then around midnight, I said, "I'm exhausted. I'm going to bed." I walked upstairs and went into my room. As soon as I walked in, I heard the Holy Spirit say, *The Lord is here.*

I sensed immediately the overwhelming presence of the King of the universe. I never saw Him with my physical eyes, but I know He was in that room. In response, I fairly screeched, *"Please don't scare me! Please don't scare me! Please don't scare me!"* The room seemed as light as a feather. I felt as though I weighed an ounce.

A couple of minutes went by, and I heard a knock at the door. It was Matt. He walked into the room and said, "The Lord is in here." Tears started welling in his eyes, and he looked scared to death. By that time I had calmed down.

Matt sat down and we stared at each other for a second. Even though it seems strange, we both knew that the Lord had sat down on the corner of the bed. Again, I am sure you think I have lost my mind and am the weirdest person you have heard of lately. Matt asked me to pray for him and I thought, *You should get* Him *to pray for you*. But I began to pray for Matt, and we both knew the moment the Lord walked out of the room. For one thing, the atmosphere changed instantly. We were stunned by this experience. I know it sounds hard to believe, but it happened.

Again, we did not see any manifestation of His presence with our fleshly eyes. It was as though we could see with the eyes of our spirits. It was not like the biblical stories of the Lord strolling into the room with Thomas or walking along with the two headed for Emmaus. Yet our hearts burned as they reported theirs did.

Why was He there that night? I honestly think that He visited us to confirm for me that I was not losing my mind and becoming some nut chasing after nothingness. On the back of one of Matt's CDs, he wrote a thank-you note to me and added, "He was there." It was so natural that it seems odd to call it supernatural.

As I have been writing this book, I have asked Jesus quite a few times why He has me doing what I am doing. I am still in process as much as anyone I know. I am getting ready to go back into counseling to work through a couple of areas in my life. But even though we are all in process, we still have the ability and the opportunity to experience the King in ways beyond just reading about Him. We need to watch, however, that "processing" does not become an excuse to sit and do nothing. That kind of *processing* becomes *unbelief* if we sit in it for too long.

Childlike curiosity and innocence open a whole new realm to followers of Jesus. People who oppose experiences in the

Kingdom would have been miserable following Jesus while He was here. It is unwise to chase experiences; however, when you walk in intimacy with someone, it is normal to share experiences together. Never having a close experience with someone you say you are intimate with would be strange.

One day I was speaking at a church that had brought its people together for a few days of refreshing. During the prayer time, a woman walked up to me and said, "Chad, I want so badly to believe in what you are saying about how real God is and how much He loves me. I just doubt it so much. I don't know what I believe anymore."

I gave her a big hug and said, "Why don't we pray?" I usually do not close my eyes when I pray, but this time I did. Her teenage daughter was standing beside her. I asked God to show her how real He is, and I spoke some thoughts out loud about His kindness.

When I opened my eyes, I saw that she was covered with what looked like gold specks. My first thought was, *This ought to be interesting.* Her daughter's eyes glanced from the specks to me and back to the specks.

I said quickly, "You know what? It's obvious that God just showed you how real He is." We continued talking together quietly, and she was able to process that experience as an example of His presence with her.

As I thought through that encounter later that day, I was intrigued because I never asked God to do that. I do not seek things like that. I was simply praying that God would show her that He is real. And He did. Signs will follow them that believe. Our role is to build friendship and intimacy with Him, and then let Him do whatever He wants.

That experience proved to me once again, by the way, how important methodology is when it comes to experiencing His presence. Being calm and gentle when things like that happen makes people around the encounter more relaxed and better able to understand what God is telling them.

## Trees and Knees

We have to get away from thinking that the supernatural is always dramatic. For me, it is calm and unassuming.

I met Brad when we both were guest speakers at a camp for teens in Bolivar, Missouri. Brad was my age, and he also traveled the country speaking to people about what it looks like to be a disciple of Jesus Christ. That night I had preached about God speaking out of the mouth of a donkey in the Old Testament (see Numbers 22:21–33). The kids laughed every time I said, "God can even speak out of the mouth of a jackass." It is funny how wild the reaction is when you say *jackass* in front of teenagers at a church camp.

Anyway, the basic premise of my sermon was that we should be open to God moving in all areas of our lives. If God can speak through a donkey, then He might not be quite so predictable. I preached with passion about not being as "safe" as we thought we were in our relationships with Jesus Christ.

When I had finished, Brad walked up to me and said, "I think you are supposed to pray for me." He told me that he had torn the ligaments in his knee playing soccer. It was painful for him to walk.

I agreed to pray for him, and we found a place to sit behind the stage. Before I began to pray, I put my hand on Brad's knee and told it to get well. Then I told him to stop moving it around. Tears filled his eyes and he said, "That's not me doing that."

Brad and I watched as his knee was healed right before our eyes. There was something moving in his ankle, and that got healed, too. The whole thing lasted about one minute.

The funny thing is that I never spoke a verbal prayer to the Father. What I did was tell Brad's knee to get well. I did that because when we sat down Jesus brought to my mind the time He told a fig tree to shrivel up. What seems weird to some seems normal to heaven. On the earth, people say, "Stay away from the nut who speaks to knees." From heaven, Jesus says, "Speak to that knee. Tell it to get better."

Most people at the camp were not aware of what had happened. The whole experience was subversive, gentle, unassuming and normal. The next day I watched Brad run a few miles on a treadmill. His wife did not know what to say. I called Wendy and said, "It's incredible what happens when you do what Jesus tells you to do."

I realized something important that night. Jesus never told His disciples to *pray for* the sick: He told them to *heal* the sick. Is that an insignificant difference? Maybe not. I have been with people who prayed long and laborious prayers over others, and nothing seemed to happen—not even in their hearts. Yet some people have prayed short, simple prayers with authority, and the unimaginable happened.

Jesus turned a boy's lunch into a meal for thousands, called a dead man out of a grave, opened blind eyes, walked on water, told a storm to hush up and sent Peter to get coins from a fish's mouth. We can be boring. I can be boring. Church can be boring. The Kingdom and its King are not boring.

But of all the things Jesus did, the one that gets my attention most is the time He spoke calmly to that fig tree. He did not talk to His Father and beg Him, if it was His will, to do something. He just told the fig tree to die. That is why I told Brad's knee to live. Jesus brought to my mind that passage and I did what He told me to do. It was a moment of walking in authority.

## The Place of Authority

Jesus said after His resurrection, "Behold, I have been given all authority" (Matthew 28:18). What does this mean for us?

Let's go back to the Garden for a second. Even though the earth belongs to God, He gave man dominion over it with instructions to care for it (see Genesis 1:28). So when Adam and Eve sinned, what did they forfeit to Satan?

Turn now to the gospels. Luke 4:2 tells us that Jesus was tempted by Satan for forty days. At one point the

> devil led him up to a high place and showed him in an instant all the kingdoms of the world. And he said to him, "I will give you all their authority and splendor, for it has been given to me, and I can give it to anyone I want to. So if you worship me, it will all be yours."
>
> Luke 4:5–7

This temptation was real. Satan had something that was "given to him" when Adam and Eve disobeyed God in the Garden. That "something" was man's dominion over the earth. Jesus reclaimed that dominion by His sacrificial death on the cross. Remember, Jesus said that He came to destroy the works of the enemy (see 1 John 3:8).

After His resurrection from the dead, Jesus handed out what was His to give: *authority*. Then He said, "Now, you go" (see Matthew 28:19). His followers are commanded to go and make disciples and obey everything He has commanded us to do. And what He has commanded us to do is partner with Him to release the Father's works.

As I read the Scriptures, I think that Jesus was excited to give the authority He had purchased on the cross to His disciples, for they could then go out as His ambassadors on the earth and defeat the works of the enemy.

I will never forget the day ten years ago when I said, "Jesus, what is the difference between me and Peter?" He immediately said, *Authority*. At that moment I entered a matrix and found that there was a world I knew nothing of. When I really started believing that I had been given authority to do the Father's works by my King, I started to see the Kingdom manifest quickly.

There were days I could not believe what I was learning. I had never heard of anything like a message of authority. The Kingdom of God is not a matter of talk; it is a matter of power. This is not arrogance, as though you and I did something to deserve this authority. It is about Jesus, for Jesus and with Jesus.

Yet it is simply mind-boggling that Jesus would invite us into this epic story and command us to do what He spent His time doing—which is destroying the works of the enemy. The Holy Spirit sent me to James 4:7–8 one night: "Submit yourselves, then, to God. Resist the devil, and he will flee from you. Come near to God and he will come near to you." I said, "Wait a second. You are telling me that the enemy will run in stark terror from me because of who Jesus is inside of me and the authority I have?"

A few nights later I walked into a church I had never visited to listen to a guest speaker. His name was Bill Johnson and he was a pastor from Redding, California. I did not know much about him at all at the time.

He preached a sermon on courage, and I felt as though someone was shocking me with electricity while he was talking. I was so stirred up I could have prophesied the white off of a golf ball.

If that were not enough, in this season of Jesus showing me all about authority, a man sitting beside me turned to me in the middle of Bill's sermon and said, "Son, God says that when you walk into a room, demons tremble and flee." That was all he said. The Greek word *flee* in James 4:8 means "to run in stark terror." I later found out that this man had worked with Billy Graham's team for a long time.

Jesus was making sure I got the message. That night on the way home I said, "I think I am starting to get it, Jesus. Your authority that You have given me and the fact that Your Spirit resides in me are the reasons that the enemy is terrified of me."

Jesus responded to me quickly: *You have to exercise authority.*

Bill preached on courage, Billy Graham's team member prophesied over me about the enemy fleeing from me and Jesus Himself showed me how the enemy views someone with authority—all in the same week.

Maybe we are building theologies upon our lack of experience in the things of the King because we have never sniffed the waters of obeying what He has called us to do. If it makes you nervous to think about these things, join the crowd. We all take a deep breath as we ponder what it really means to be His disciple. I bet you a hundred bucks that Peter looked at Jesus as if He were crazy when Jesus talked to that fig tree.

The first time I came across that passage I thought that Jesus did some really weird things. Yet here I am, still trying to answer the question of what it looks like to be the disciple of the One who did these weird things. The only answer I can come up with is that I must look and act like the One I am following until it becomes normal.

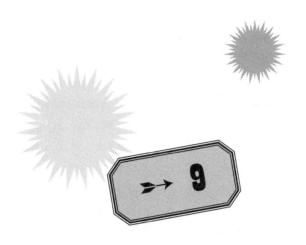

# Yada, Yada, Yada

I was eight years old and I was in love. When she walked into my second grade classroom every day, my heart would sing like a heavenly bird inside of my chest. Her name was Christy and I wanted to marry her. My dad always trained me to think big. I figured that my parents would be up for my marrying this beautiful young lady.

I had a major problem though. I clammed up and got quieter than a librarian when I was around her. No matter how much I psyched myself up, I could not bring myself to talk to her. She was sovereignly placed by God to sit in the seat beside me. Second grade was a good year.

One night at home, I decided that I could not take it anymore. I snapped. I wrote one of the most beautiful letters I have constructed in my entire life. It read like this: "Dear Christy, I love you. Do you love me? Yes, no, maybe. Please circle one." I then sprinkled some of my dad's cologne on the letter.

The next morning I put the letter on her desk. I could barely breathe. A boy became a man. The anticipation was beyond any second grader's ability to handle. I had a dream and I was waiting for the fulfillment. What happened next would be my first taste of courtship heartbreak. Christy never gave me the note back. Her family moved away and I was left to wonder what could have been. Poof. It was gone like mist in the night.

Even at a young age, I found my heart longing for friendship. It is funny (now) to look back on what I was feeling in the second grade. We all go through it. You probably remember the first time that someone caught your eye or became a special pal. While growing up, I knew that Richard Burgess was "my best friend." Even now my three-year-old Jack loves to tell people, "You are my best friend." It seems as though we have something built in us by God Himself that desires to connect to others in deep friendship.

We want to know and be known, to be intimate with another person in friendship. I wish I had known as a child that we long to have this kind of relationship with God as well.

That is what I want to ponder in this chapter—knowing the Father. What does it mean—not only after we die, but right now, today? Let's start with the basics. What does it mean to know, really know, someone?

## Getting to Know You

When I started dating Wendy, my heart was beating for more than just conversations about how her classes were going. There comes a point when a 22-year-old male wants to do more than hold his fiancée's hand.

Yes, I am talking about sex. The Church has an opportunity to define sexuality in healthy ways. The Creator of the world invented it. It is fun. It is normal. It is pure. It is heaven's agenda for married couples. After being married for fifteen years, Wendy and I have learned together as a couple that God's intention for His invention is more than just a physical act. I heard this in a marriage seminar early on, but it has taken me a while to realize that this is true.

I remember telling Wendy that we had to get married quick because I could not stay engaged to her for a long time and remain sane. It was not easy. It never is. Sometimes when you are dating someone, you feel as though you are on high alert all the time. At least, you feel this way if you are trying to honor the Lord with purity.

Why is this? I believe that our Father put something inside of us that longs for connection on a deep level beyond simply talking with the love of your life. If I ever say, "Intimacy is not my thing," I may need someone to beat me in the head with a boat paddle, because something is wrong with me. Intimacy is something God created us for. When He told Adam and Eve to go and multiply, He was not talking about a board game. He basically said, "I made both of you. Go enjoy your nakedness and have fun. Be intimate."

He wants us to have intimacy. Sex is part of this in marriage, but only part. In the Father's eyes, it is not normal to have solely a cordial relationship between spouses. He wants spouses to be close.

Likewise, He wants to be close to us. If the supernatural is something that you want to become natural in your life, you simply have to believe this. I have never met anyone who walks in the Father's works who does not understand this concept. He desires intimacy with us. It is shocking.

When we teach at our church about how to walk in these things, we start here. Intimacy with the Creator of the world will naturally lead to His Kingdom manifesting in our lives. Jesus told the God-fearing people around Him, "You do not know me or my Father" (John 8:19). Praying with authority is not about being cocky, it is about exercising His power. The authority to do so is cultivated through deep and consistent intimacy with Him.

The longer Peter lived, the more he became acquainted with the God who sent His Son—a man whom Peter walked with. Peter transitioned from a self-consumed, impulsive, fearful follower to someone whose shadow made others whole.

There is much to be discovered about the implications of walking in intimacy with God. When He becomes the lover of our souls, extending His Kingdom is not something that we have to strive to do. The first thing I tell people who want to see the Kingdom manifest is this: "Get to know Him more intimately than anyone you have ever known—through His Word, soaking in His presence, music, fellowship with other believers." When we want Him more than we want anything else in the world, we will see His works flow naturally from our walk with Him.

Have you ever considered that your intimacy with God could be the breakthrough someday for someone you have never even met? He is not asking us to memorize powerful prayers. He is asking us to walk in intimacy with Him. That is what Jesus did. He was always seeking seclusion from the crowds in order to be with His Father. Jesus grew in wisdom and favor (see Luke 2:52). So should we.

Jesus talked about hearing the voice of His Father. He gave us a perfect example of what it looks like when one person is completely abandoned to this idea of intimacy with God Almighty.

This is what the LORD says: "Let not the wise boast of their wisdom or the strong boast of their strength or the rich boast of their riches, but let the one who boasts boast about this: that they have the understanding to know me, that I am the LORD, who exercises kindness, justice and righteousness on earth, for in these I delight," declares the LORD.

Jeremiah 9:23–24

Jeremiah said that if we boast about anything we should boast that we know God. What does that mean?

## A Sneak Peek

I cannot tell you how many times in seminary I said, "I would rather be attacked by a wild llama than be in this Hebrew class." I hated studying Hebrew. For one thing, I was terrible at it. Where other people saw letters formed in the lines and curves on their pages, I seemed to be staring at one gigantic, chaotic mess. So it is funny that God took one teeny-weeny little Hebrew word and used it to flip my world upside down.

One day while studying in my office at work, I decided to track down the meaning of the word that my Bible translated as "know." What did Jeremiah mean by "knowing" God?

The answer for me was the Hebrew word *yada*. The only time I had ever heard *yada* was when I would hear someone say, "Yada, Yada, Yada," to describe someone else who would not shut up. But learning this word made me feel as if I had gone through that little rabbit hole in *Alice in Wonderland*.

Eight years later, I am still searching for the fullness of this little word. In Hebrew, *yada* is not just about head knowledge of God. It describes intimate connection to Him. This same Hebrew word is used in Genesis 4:1, which says that "Adam knew Eve his wife; and she conceived" (KJV). Let that sink in for a second. A child is conceived when man is with woman in the most intimate act.

So what in the world was Jeremiah talking about here when he said we should know God? Obviously he was not being gross or indecent. Instead, God is telling us through His prophet that He loves it when we walk in close intimacy with Him. By learning this word, I got revelation that this God, who I thought was mad at me, actually wanted to walk in intimacy with me. This one word, *yada*, opened my eyes to the possibility that there was a deeper expression of experiential intimacy with God. I wanted to explore it fully.

Now I tie everything that I have learned back to this concept. Everything that we receive from the Father comes from our intimacy with Him. Extreme intimacy with the Father makes the enemy incredibly nervous—even terrified. Actually, I spend very little time—if any—thinking about what the enemy is up to. The goal is to get as close to the Father as possible. So in these verses, Jeremiah gives us a sneak peek into what Jesus talked about. Building a deep friendship with God is the ultimate pursuit. I started to think about the idea that sheep really have only one job.

They need to stay close to the shepherd and keep their eyes on him.

As I began my study of this word in my office, I literally said out loud: "Let me get this straight—I can talk to You as a man talks to his friend? I can seriously talk to You and learn to hear Your voice and know You closely?" God said yes.

At first I wondered how I would distinguish God's voice from mine. I thought the whole thing was crazy. Yet the further I went down the rabbit hole, the more I realized that there was a Kingdom life that I knew nothing about. One day, during this time, I was writing a check for our monthly mortgage payment, and I heard, *Don't write that.* Somehow I knew it was God speaking to me. I could not deny it. I wrote the check anyway, only to realize a week later that Wendy had already written one.

Perhaps God is closer than we think. Perhaps He enjoys being part of even the small details of our lives. I know that many people who are very serious about God may want to throw up when they read what I have just written because it seems small and childish. But I think that being childish might lead us to a world we would never otherwise consider.

## Learning about Intimacy

Mama Jane used to take me fishing when I was a kid. Even now, I can close my eyes and smell the Georgia air as it came across my uncle Jack's pond. We never fished for bass because Mama Jane always wanted to fish for bream. I put live crickets on my hook and tossed my line out into the calm waters. Those times felt like perfection to me.

It was not the water. It was not how the fish were biting. It was my grandmother. She actually talked to me and asked me how I was doing and what I wanted for dinner that night. She listened to me and gave me advice on how to fish well. It was just the two of us sitting in the same boat enjoying each other. Sometimes I sat in her lap. It is possible that woman never fully realized what happened inside my heart when she held me. I felt connected to her. It would take me years to figure out that my relationship with Mama Jane was a taste of what is available to me with the God of the universe.

In Haiti one afternoon, God said to me, *You still don't know how kind I am. Why is it so easy for you to think of the kindness of Mama Jane, but you still have a hard time thinking of Me as kind?*

People ask me all of the time if I am charismatic. I used to respond by asking, "What do you mean by that statement?" These days I answer by saying, "God is now my Father, and I like Him a lot. That is what I am."

If you think charismatic things make people feel uncomfortable, try telling them that you are intimate with the Maker of heaven and earth. But more and more, all over the world, people are becoming intimate with the Father. Things that used to be considered charismatic are becoming normal. That is because the supernatural is not about putting on a show—or even about expressing a belief system. It comes from a deep intimate connection between a person and God.

Have you noticed that Jesus called God "Father" most of the time? Almost always—until He got to the cross. The religious establishment got incredibly aggravated when Jesus talked about His Father. (See John 8, for example.)

Recently I went to a conference with more than ten thousand people in attendance. The speakers, who are well-known preachers and teachers, used the word *Father* only once or twice during the whole conference. It seems odd to me that we follow God's Son but hardly ever refer to God the way Jesus did. Jesus' vocabulary was full of the word *Father*; that is how Jesus knew Him.

Do you refer to God as "Father"? If not, open a door in your heart and ask Him to show you why not. I think that part of the reason so many people do not call God "Father" is that they had pathetic examples in their own fathers. As a result, it is difficult for them to consider that God could be different from what they have seen modeled, and they are not eager to replicate that experience.

Calling God "Father" instead of "God" may seem like a small difference, but in reality it is as wide as an ocean. You can tell a lot about a person by how he or she refers to God. As I have said, Jesus referred to God as His Father, and called His miracles the works of His Father. Jesus operated with power, and it flowed out of this intimate connection.

But as stirring as that was, maybe the most stunning thing Jesus said was to call God "Abba." I want to show you why this was such a bombshell to His listeners.

## Abba Who?

I have an obsession with the disciples. These guys were so stinking real that it is not even funny. They had front-row seats to the most astonishing story of all time, and they were basically clueless. Of the many head-scratching times the disciples experienced during their three years with Jesus, the one that stands out to me as probably most challenging for them was Jesus' revelation about God.

Put yourself in their shoes. Their baseline about God, taken from centuries—millennia—of careful religious training, established Him as unapproachable. They knew all the Bible stories of God's refusal to compromise. (We have already noted how Aaron's two sons brought "unholy fire" to the altar of sacrifice and got smoked.) God told His people, recorded in Exodus 19:22, that if the priests did not consecrate themselves, they would get it, too. God just did not seem very nice. His holiness was uncomfortable.

Nor did He seem approachable. Moses wanted badly to see God (see Exodus 33:18–23), but God said that Moses could view only His back as He passed by. When you think of God in the Old Testament, the chances of connecting with Him intimately seem remote.

So when Jesus called God "Abba," we can imagine Peter saying something like, "Jesus, let me get this straight. What I hear You saying is that You are God's Son. Even though You grew up in a very average town that never produces anything good, and even though Your parents are Mary and Joseph, You are telling me that from now on, You want me to get to know Your Father—who is God—as my Father, and call Him *Abba*?"

I think we read the Bible so fast sometimes that we fail to ponder what we are reading. It would be as awkward for Andrew and Thomas to call God "Daddy" as it would be for you to go grocery shopping naked. But this miracle-working carpenter's Son, this unlikely rabbi, talked about calling the thundering God of the world "Daddy."

I think many of us have been taught to turn God's image into something we can be comfortable with and manage well. I can promise you one thing: I never once thought of calling God "Daddy" when I was younger. One time in my youth group a girl called Him "Daddy" in a prayer, and we all laughed at her. Several of us even tried to get her to move to the crazy church down the street where she would fit in better. Little did I know that she understood something that would take me years to discover. So I can relate to Andrew, Thomas, Luke and those others who would have looked at Jesus as though He were a crazy person.

When is the last time you called God "Daddy"? Let's take it one step further and use the word *Da-da*. The word *Abba* in Aramaic is extremely intimate in the way *Da-da* is. Even now, if you go to Jerusalem you will hear little children saying "Abba, Abba" as they talk to their dads.

## Three Little Rascals

My three children, Sam, Ruthie and Jack, have a couple of similarities and a ton of differences.

Sam has been called an "old soul." He is the nine-year-old who sits on the front porch and talks about the good ol' days. He is tenderhearted, loyal and responsible. It sounds funny to call your nine-year-old son one of your best friends, but that is exactly how I see Sam. It would not surprise me at all to work with Sam the rest of my life. He travels with me, hangs out with me and helps raise the other two. He is a good companion.

Ruthie, six, is my passionate one. Ruthie is stubborn, zealous and determined, yet she is sweet, adorable and thoughtful.

She wants to know where the boundaries are. She may or may not cross them, but she always wants to know exactly where they are so that she can decide. She is the one that I can be laughing with one second and crying with the next. I see Jesus in Ruthie's eyes. Recently I have noticed this more and more and I think she teaches me more about Him than I do her. I love how Ruthie brings excitement to our house. She has never had a boring day.

Jack, three, is one of a kind. I probably have never met anyone like Jack. He is funny, gregarious and wild to the core. It is no big deal to walk into the bathroom and find Jack attempting a handstand with his head in the commode. Whereas Ruthie will test the boundaries, Jack knows no boundaries. One day at a golf course, I decided to let him walk as far as he would go simply to see where he ended up. He got 150 yards away from me before he finally turned around. He loves to wrestle, eat Cheetos and hit stuff. We call him Jack-Jack because his personality is so big he deserves to have his name said twice. He is the one who has the biggest potential to send me back on medication.

Sam, Ruthie and Jack are three children with three different personalities, but they share one major theme: As their daddy, I would do anything for them to bless their lives. That is exactly the way that our Abba, our Daddy, looks at us. This thought has changed everything for me. The grace of Jesus has a hard time flowing in our lives when we fail to understand how much our Father loves us. When we can grasp this concept, we will live holier lives by accident than we ever could by trying without that revelation. Satan has distorted the true heart of God. From the very beginning, God has always wanted the best for His people. Look back to Genesis 12:1–3 and see for yourself.

It is not just a theological exercise to think thoughts like this. If you do not have a deep revelation of how kind God is, you will find it nearly impossible to see major breakthroughs when you pray for people. If you are where I was and you are tired of not seeing the Kingdom manifest in your life more, start focusing your mind on His kindness, forgiveness and unconditional love. Then start praying for people.

It is impossible to describe what is in my heart toward my children. I love them. How do you describe love? There are no words. All I know is that a father's love is real and deep. Jesus is an exact representation of His Father. It is too good to be true.

## Daddy's Home!

The scene is almost always the same when I come home from work. The boys are going about their business. Sam is watching TV or doing homework. Jack is tearing up something.

Ruthie, however, is locked and loaded and ready for assault. Whether I have been gone for five minutes or five days, when I walk through that door, my daughter runs straight at me and screams "Daddy!" She jumps up into my arms and squeezes me tight. I have equally strong connections with Sam and Jack, but my connection with Ruthie is different. Not better; just different. It touches a special place in my heart. When I drive up in the driveway I anticipate my baby girl running right at me. Just the other night, I was shopping with Ruthie and she looked up at me and said, "I love you, Daddy." I wanted to sit down and cry. I never get tired of hearing that.

But every once in a while when I come home, Ruthie is nowhere in sight. And when she is not bounding toward me, I notice. I miss it. That is because I love it when one of my children calls me "Daddy." Sam does not call me "Daddy"; he calls me "Dad." Jack usually grunts at me. But not Ruthie. My girl calls me "Daddy."

Now, if I phoned my own father right now and called him "Daddy," he would ask me if I were okay. He would probably think that I was on something, to be honest with you, because a grown man typically does not call his father "Daddy"; it sounds so intimate. And that probably explains why you hardly ever hear anyone call God "Father," much less "Abba" or "Daddy."

I believe God gets a ton of glory when one of His children refers to Him with the term that He told His Son to tell us to call Him. The disciples struggled with this concept, but Paul seemed to have a better revelation about it. Paul used the word *Abba* in Galatians 4:6. Paul was not someone you would call a "feeler." As a matter of fact, Paul lived as one of the most driven, unfeeling personalities I have ever read about. Yet after he met Jesus, he joined in teaching us to relate to God as Daddy.

Right now I have a man crush on Paul. I never really paid that much attention to him compared to my obsession with Simon Peter and John. Those two usually claim most of my attention for whatever reason. But right now, Paul fascinates me.

Paul, an extremist, protected the Jewish lifestyle, and he killed Christians to do it. He was a big deal. Then one day out of nowhere, Jesus knocked him down, and everything changed. Paul stopped denying Jesus and began preaching

His message about Abba. He even raised the dead on the side.

Paul *got it*. He understood that trying to walk in the power of God without knowing Abba is useless striving. It produces tones that are no more melodic than a clanging gong.

Most people fear that walking in intimacy with Abba means being embarrassingly emotional. But remember: Paul told us that the Kingdom of God is not a matter of talk but of power. In other words, we cannot live in power without a revelation of Abba. If we want more of His power working in our lives, we do not need to focus on faith; we need to focus on intimacy with the Creator of the world. As I have said, we have more problems with love and intimacy than we have with faith. Faith operates by love (see Galatians 5:6).

If I never refer to God as "Father," "Abba" or "Daddy," then I need seriously to evaluate whether I have gotten to know God through His Word or through other sources. I recently listened to a very popular preacher and the whole time he was preaching I thought, *He is presenting God as one of the most miserable people I have ever heard of.*

Paul was not vague about this. He burned for one thing: to know Father, Son and Holy Spirit as intimately as possible. Check out what Paul said at the end of his life: "I want to know Christ and the power of His resurrection" (Philippians 3:10). This word *know* suggests deep, intimate, experiential connection with someone.

Does that sound familiar? It sounds a lot like *yada* in Hebrew. What is God saying here? That He wants a deep abiding friendship with you and me that starts on this earth and takes us in to eternity. For the early hearers of this text, the mindset of God was not one of "close, intimate" connection.

Adam and Eve walked intimately with Him from the very beginning. When Jesus came to earth, He reconnected His followers with the idea of God's desire to walk closely with His people. One day this dawned on me: "Wait a minute, God sent Jesus here and then chose to reside inside of His people." He wants to be close to us.

Some years back, I was concerned about what others thought of me when I talked about things like this. I would seek Abba in the privacy of my own home, but I would really tone down my language in public. It was a little embarrassing to call Him "Daddy" in front of others—and I wanted their affirmation. The fear of man is a powerful motivator.

Finally, I got to the point where I did not care anymore. If Jesus called Him "Father" or "Abba," then I was going to pursue Him in the same way. And as I got to know my Abba, I started to see Him do some incredible things.

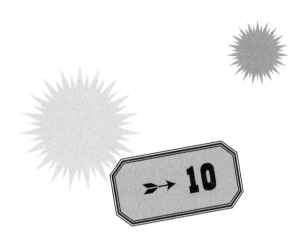

# Hosting His Presence

As a kid growing up I lived for two things: macaroni and cheese and weekends. For me, getting a weekend was like an adult getting an inheritance. I used to run out of school on Friday afternoons with extra excitement because I knew what was awaiting me. During the week my mom made my brother, sister and me eat healthful meals, but on the weekends we got to eat anything that we wanted. It was almost too much for my senses to take in.

In the fall, Friday nights meant high school football, and Saturday afternoons meant college football. It was heaven on a stick—until Saturday night. On Saturday night, my body tensed with stress because of what would happen the next morning—church socks.

Can I ask a question? Why did so many of us grow up in church cultures where our parents made us wear the most uncomfortable clothes on the planet? On Saturdays I wore my football jersey, jeans and a baseball cap. On Sundays I wore pants made of scratchy wool, socks that made me itch, and a tie so tight I wanted to punch someone in the face. No wonder kids did not like going to church back in the day. We were miserable because of what we were wearing.

One day at the dinner table after church, I told my mom, "I bet you a thousand bucks that Jesus Christ did not wear these socks." I complained about how my feet were swollen and itching. She told me to be quiet and eat my fried chicken.

I mentioned to someone recently that I cannot believe how much I enjoy church. That person responded that I have to come whether I enjoy it or not—since I am on staff. I thought that was funny because he is right. But I was telling the truth. Our church has a culture where I can actually go after the things that my King went after while He was here. I can attempt to teach the Kingdom, pray healing over people and drive the enemy out of people's lives. I cannot name many places that would allow me to do all three. The Father has been good to me.

As a Pastor of Life Transformation at our church, I get the opportunity to teach and preach often. As you have read, I lead our initiative to Haiti to partner with Bethel Mission Outreach. But what happens on Monday nights is the place where we see so many of our Father's works manifest. You never know what is going to happen at Hosting His Presence.

In layman's terms, Hosting His Presence is a healing and intercession service that is not weird. Most of the time when you hear the words *healing service*, you think of something that is flashy, loud or showy. Hosting His Presence is nothing like that. Our services last from 6:30–8:00 p.m. We have worship in the main auditorium where people "soak" in His presence.

Sometimes I will teach for a little bit, or someone else will teach, or sometimes there will be no teaching at all. Sometimes we simply intercede for our city and what we are sensing that the Father wants us to address strategically in prayer. In the back, we have healing rooms set up. Our church has some sixty people who are trained to pray for the sick and broken. Over the past seven years of offering this service, we have heard testimony after testimony of healing. And there is an increase in what we are seeing manifest.

Let me give you an example. Recently I saw a student from Clemson University receive a wonderful touch of healing power as we prayed for her eczema. She felt heat flow all over her body. The itching on her scalp lessened, and she was overcome with the kindness and gentleness of Abba. That is just one example. I could go on and on about the different healings that are taking place.

People do not come in solely for healing; they also come to the prayer rooms for prophetic words. We love it when people receive words from heaven for their lives. I have seen many people weep when they realize how much Abba really cares about them. We train our people to bless others with what the Father is saying. The gentleness of heaven is amazing to watch as people come off the streets and later leave realizing for the first time in their lives that the heavenly realm is closer than they thought.

The fun thing about Hosting His Presence is that the people leading in the prayer rooms are not paid ministers. They are just normal people with their own normal problems who release tiny faith and see huge breakthroughs.

Rich, who is the lead pastor at our church, came up with the idea for this service. His thought was simple: "Host His Presence and get out of the way." I sometimes try to make it more complicated than that, but it is truly that simple. People who are broken drive to this service from many miles away now because of one thing: His Presence.

Hosting His Presence is designed, in fact, for the sake of our city. Every denomination you can think of is represented in the participants. It is always amusing when people tell us they came to spy on us only to discover that Hosting His Presence is nothing like they thought it would be. Other churches in our area often send their prayer teams to our Prayer Servant classes to be trained to pray for people with grace and dignity and the expectation that the impossible will happen.

In the past few years I have begun to ask people who come for healing this question: "If I could somehow get us back two thousand years to when Jesus was in the Middle East, and we went to one of His healing meetings, do you think He would heal you?" Very rarely does someone say no; most people say yes immediately. This is a simple question that seems to affect people on an emotive level. I cannot tell you how many times I have heard, "I never thought about it that way." Does everyone we pray for receive healing? Of course not. We just choose to keep moving forward no matter what the results are.

Healing and prophetic words seem strained and difficult if we think about Jesus up in heaven somewhere—but not when we picture Him standing right beside us. And that is the reality. The Word says that His presence is inside of us (see Galatians 2:20). If He is inside of me, maybe I just need to believe it, act like it and pray like it.

Before I pray for any healing or miracle for someone I say the same thing: "Jesus, You are inside of me, and You are quite capable of helping this person." The first few times I felt heat flow from my hands I freaked out. Now it is no big deal.

One of my favorite Scriptures is this: "Never will I leave you; never will I forsake you" (Hebrews 13:5). Jesus is a lot closer to us than we think. If you have trouble believing me, just try laying your hands on your friend's head the next time he or she has a headache. This approach to prayer is calm, relaxed and fun. Old Testament-era priests had to wear white linen because they were not supposed to sweat. Neither are we. Just pray calmly and trust the One who lives inside of you rather than yourself. You will actually be doing what His first disciples did.

As I train people to pray for the sick and broken, I usually remind them that Jesus is not deaf. When I first started walking in these things years ago, I prayed for a woman, and I heard the Lord say to me, *Why are you being so loud?* I got the point. The reason many of us do not see signs and wonders happen on a consistent basis is that we simply do not believe we can pray and get results. So we make up for lack of belief with volume.

## Gentle Prayers and Quiet Answers

I have asked the Lord approximately a million times to send me a DVD showing Him healing people. After a few years of praying this, I had a dream the night before I started working full-time at City Church. In the dream, I was in the basement of the large Baptist church I grew up in. There were fifteen or so people there, and I was telling them about my out-of-the-box experiences with the Lord.

All of a sudden, I turned around to see the Lord standing there. His beard looked unkempt, and He had on a common white tunic. Seven severely diseased and mangled people stood near Him. He went to them one by one and gently touched their heads with His hand, and they were healed. The Lord never took His eyes off of me while He did this.

I was scared to death in my dream. I did not know what to do. Then the Lord smiled, and I knew that He was showing me what it looked like when He prayed for people.

I remembered that on the night I call "The Burrito Breakthrough." I had just finished speaking to a group of students and a few of the leaders headed out for burritos after the service. As I was standing in line contemplating the euphoria that my taste buds were about to experience from the flaming hot sauce that this restaurant was famous for, a man tapped me on the shoulder. He said, "Do you remember tonight when you said that you love to pray for anyone at anytime for anything?"

My mind was still occupied with the burrito headed my way, but I nodded and said, "Of course, what is going on?"

He told me that he was struggling to quit smoking. He said he was coughing a lot and his lungs did not feel right. He then asked me, "Do you think Jesus will help me even though I am struggling with cigarettes?"

If he had asked me that question a dozen years ago, I am not sure what I would have said. This night, however, I looked right at him and assured him. "One of the biggest shocks of my life," I said, "was when I realized how tender and loving God truly is." I reminded him about the passage where Jesus does not condemn the woman caught in the act of adultery (see John 8:1–11). That passage seemed to open this man's eyes to the idea that perhaps even in the midst of his own struggle, Jesus was not obsessed with it, nor was He looking to punish him for his shortcomings.

We sat down with our burritos and prayed, asking Jesus to heal him. The man said he could not believe the immediate difference he felt. He could breathe with no pain for the first time in months. We continued to talk and enjoy our meal.

I have not heard from him since that night. I do not know if smoking is a part of his life anymore. The way in which I look at this situation is that it was not my job to condemn him but to show the love of the Father to him. I can assure you that he will not forget the kindness of God's touch anytime soon. Neither will I. For the record, the burrito was delicious.

Let me mention here that I think our church sees so many people healed because we put all of the pressure on the Lord. I am sure that if you ask five ministries that operate in Kingdom power how they go about it you would get five different answers. For us, we have chosen to focus on who Jesus is in us, and then submit the problem to His ability to handle it. This may seem simplistic, but we have seen many people experience freedom. Whether I am praying for someone who is dying or someone with a toothache, I pray the same way.

If you find yourself getting nervous about praying for others, it might be because you think you are the one responsible. People many times look at those who walk in Kingdom power and say, "That woman is so arrogant" or "Who does that man think he is?" The truth is often the opposite. Our prayer team simply prays with the faith of a child. We are aware of our own shortcomings and brokenness. That is one of the beautiful things about the Kingdom. God loves to use simple, unassuming and oftentimes scared people to do His works.

A couple of years ago, some of our team members went to the hospital to visit a teenage girl in our church who was fighting for her life. Right before we walked into the hospital room, we reminded ourselves that Jesus does the healing and that the power is His, not ours. I said, "Lord, I'm a little scared right now, but this is no big deal to You."

As we entered the room of that young lady, I thought how the color of her skin was the color a body turns right before death. I looked around that hospital room and thought, *Jesus, all things are possible with You. All things are possible with You.*

I could tell that the family was open to believing that Jesus would help their daughter. I touched her gently and we prayed a simple prayer. That was it. Over the next few weeks she got dramatically better. About a year later, I was in a store and saw her working as the clerk at the counter. Jesus is good.

If you are in a place right now where you would never consider going into a hospital room and praying for someone in really bad shape, you are not in such a bad place. Take it easy on yourself. As a matter of fact, I believe that fear can actually drive us closer to God Himself as we pray for others.

Trust me, if you could be in community with me, you would not say, "Oh, Chad is so spiritual and deep. I could never be like him." Rather, I guarantee that you would say, "Hmmm. If God can use Chad, then I know He can use me." The more I walk with this idea of being naturally supernatural, the more I am convinced that God loves using normal, everyday-type people to do His gentle works.

## Theology and Methodology

Sometimes people who are skeptical of the supernatural realm have the opportunity to witness God's power at work in our church or through one of our ministry teams. Many times they see someone get healed or delivered from the enemy and say, "Oh, that was real—and it wasn't obnoxious," or words to that effect.

I understand this. As I began to grow in intimacy with the Lord, I kept telling Him, "Lord, I love You, but I don't want to be odd. I'll do anything for You. Just don't make me look like an idiot."

The reason people are skeptical about signs and wonders today is not the miracles themselves; it is the way Jesus has been represented in the Western culture. For some reason, we pay more attention to how people misrepresent the King than we do to how the King operated. In other words, I believe that the Lord cares not only about theology, but also about methodology—the "how" of ministry, the "what it looks like." We do not have to look like idiots in order to obey the Father.

Any hesitation about things of the Spirit is a sign that we do not understand the "how" of Jesus' ministry. What did it look like? What was His methodology?

My favorite definition of *theology* came from Fisher Humphries, my theology professor at Beeson Divinity School. He said, "Theology is thinking about God." I love reading books that stretch my theology. I love learning. I love growing in deeper revelation of who God is.

I also love *methodology*. Again, I believe that bad methodology is the reason so many people disdain signs and wonders today. It is not primarily a theological issue; it is primarily a methodological issue. Simply put, most of us do not feel comfortable with *the way* in which people walk in the things of the supernatural.

If this is the case, then it follows that charismatic events are not really the problem; we are the problem. Someone needs to demonstrate that you do not have to be strange in order to see a person healed. When we at City Church pray for people at times, you could be ten feet away and not know that we are praying for healing. In fact, if you see someone calling attention to him or herself, perhaps that one is not speaking for the Lord.

## Doing His (Gentle) Works

As I get older, I hear many more people speak about not only what God is showing them in their studies but also what He is showing them in the "everydayness" of their lives when it comes to seeing the Kingdom manifest. Demonstration is accompanying proclamation. Even from unlikely circles.

This is a great thing. More and more people are welcoming the idea of God breaking through. Perhaps this change is not happening because theology is different; it is happening because methodology is different.

John 14:12 is not gray. It is not confusing. It says, "Whoever believes in me will do the works I have been doing, and they will do even greater things than these, because I am going to the Father." People are learning that Kingdom power is not about "the great man of God" who rides into town with great faith. It is about the common man with just a little bit of faith who starts to do the things that Jesus did. How do I know? I see it every week of my life.

Hosting His Presence is not about anything other than inviting Jesus to do what He loved doing while He was here. We have seen sickness leave, marriages be restored, addicts get delivered and give their lives to Jesus, migraines vanish, blind eyes open, broken bones knit together, depression lift, people get delivered of demons and more.

One of our goals at the start of the ministry was to help create a place where we not only pray for people but also have time to soak in His presence. We felt that it would prepare our hearts to receive from our Savior if we spent time worshiping Him first. Simultaneously, we discovered that the act of intercession was growing stronger. It was obvious that God was beginning to move differently.

In our city, other churches are also hosting Abba's presence and seeing what will happen when they pray for impossible things. Methodist, Presbyterian and Baptist churches are sharing testimonies of our Father bringing wholeness to people the same way He did with His Son, Jesus.

There is an 84-year-old woman in our church named Loraine. Some people here prayed for her, and she was healed of spinal stenosis. I was not there but when I heard the story I laughed and said, "Jesus is too good to be true." It is never too late to taste the Kingdom of God on the earth. She had severe pain and Jesus Christ healed her. I love hugging her neck on Sunday mornings. Her simple love for Jesus is intoxicating.

## Climbing Out of the Boat

One night the twelve disciples were in a boat. It was storming at sea, and the boys were scared. Then their Rabbi came walking on the water. Peter called out, "If that's you, tell me to come out there with you" (see Matthew 14:28).

Jesus said, "Come," and Peter walked on the water. Note that the other eleven disciples did not. All thirteen men could have been walking on that water, yet only two of them were.

I will tell you this: I still have my diapers on when I compare my life to the disciples' lives. Peter walked on water; the time I tried, I sank faster than a bowling ball. This occurred because one day beside a pond a while back I told Jesus: "If Peter could walk on water, then I have a fighting chance." I crashed through that water so stinking fast.

But the point is this: I was beginning to think along the lines of John 14:12. Now, let me add that I spent eighteen years in Christ and not one soul experienced a supernatural touch from Jesus through my hands. That has not been the case these last ten years. What changed? I can only conclude that I started taking His command more seriously. The time comes when you have to say, "I don't care if I drown, but I cannot stay in this boat any longer." I have a long way to go, but at least I am taking a hack at emulating my King.

What about you? I dare you to get out of the boat and post a Facebook status of a time and place that you will pray for anyone who wants prayer. I dare you to get out of the boat and start a prayer ministry at your church where you and your friends pray for impossible things to happen. Being scared is okay. We all get scared. Choose to move past your fear.

Jesus said, "You are my friends if you do what I command" (John 15:14). That one stings a little bit. Perhaps millions of us will be in shock one day when we get to heaven and He says, "I've always loved you. Why didn't you do the things I commanded you to do in the Scriptures?" When people come to me and tell me that God is not calling them to do the things that our church is doing, I have to say that I feel confused. He gave us these commands a long, long time ago. Is it not a matter of believing what He has already said for us to do? Is Scripture not enough? Do we need a new call?

I love the response of the blind man whom Jesus healed. He said, "Look, I don't understand it either, but now I can see" (see John 9:1–11). I want those unexplainable things happening in my life every week. This is not a matter of competency. None of us ever gets to the place of figuring out how in the world the Father's power can flow through tiny little people like us. We are all aware that nothing inside of us besides Him is capable of doing anything. It is simply a matter of obedience and courage.

Instead of generating theories about why prayer "works" or "does not work," we should be doing what He has already told us to do. This is heaven's invitation to us.

## Overcoming Fear

The reason that Satan spends so much time prompting us to fear is that he is the biggest coward of all. I have known fear with the best of them. I have walked through many seasons in which fear was my closest friend. Then I got to a point where I realized that the opposite of fear is not faith. The opposite of fear is love. When we learn to accept love from the Father, we can exercise faith even in the midst of our fear.

One night early in my journey of seeking the Kingdom, I woke up around three a.m. to the most dreadful feeling I can describe. My wife is not a crier, but she woke up screaming at the top of her lungs. Sam, who was just a year old at the time, also woke up screaming. I heard the Lord's voice in my right ear say, *It's Satan.* It all happened so fast. Earlier that week, the Lord had told me that I was going to come under serious scrutiny from Satan. I figured He meant through other people.

The feeling of evil in that room was remarkable. I never saw anything that night with my physical eyes, yet it was real. I have never been more terrified in my life. Evil was in our room. I was not full of faith at that moment. I was scared to death.

So I did the only thing I knew to do. I called out, "Jesus!" My wife and I both experienced an instant change from evil and cold to the peace of Jesus. The peace of heaven surrounded us. It happened instantly. When I yelled the name *Jesus*, it was like flipping on a switch.

I know exactly why Satan was there in our room. I was just beginning to walk in the supernatural, and he was trying to scare me to death. I knew fear that night, but I chose to exercise my faith—even though at the time I felt as though I had none—and continue doing the works of Jesus. My plan is to imitate my Big Brother and destroy the works of Satan all over this globe.

Faith is simply moving forward and punching fear in the mouth. Was I afraid that night? Beyond what I can describe. Even now as I process what happened and try to follow Jesus with my life, I deal with fear. I have never met anyone who does not struggle with fear at times. If you wait until all fear is gone from your heart, you will never (and I mean never) have the courage to do the works of the Father.

But there is another way. The Bible says that "perfect love drives out fear" (1 John 4:18). The more that we saturate our minds with how much the Father loves us, the less we will find ourselves afraid. Deep intimacy with Him and His love for us produce faith.

More and more Christians are starting to wonder: When are the Stephens going to start roaming the halls of our schools? Where are all the Philips and Andrews? When are our shadows going to bring the Kingdom here? Honestly, the day of the Father's works is upon us, and normal people like you and me should be getting fed up with powerless Christianity.

When a Spirit-filled person shows up with the revelation of who she really is and how much she is loved, the enemy quakes in his boots. One time I was reading the story of David and Goliath and I heard the Lord say, *Who killed Goliath?*

My thought process went as follows: David slung the rock, but God killed Goliath. It was the power of God that took the giant down—but David had to throw the rock. I kept going. Noah built the boat. Moses spoke to Pharaoh. Esther approached Xerxes, and so on. God loves to use people to fulfill His purposes. It is His gunpowder, but He asks us to pull the trigger. Joshua was scared but he entered the Promised Land and began his battles. Even though the river might be raging, sometimes you simply have to step into it and trust that God will do what only He can do.

Until you have seen a demon-possessed person fall at your feet because of who lives in you, it is hard to understand. That is what happened when Jesus walked into to a cemetery where a madman was terrorizing people. The madman knelt before the King. That King's Spirit is now in us, and the underworld knows that better than most Christians.

We are not powerless. We are not pathetic. No, we carry the presence of a terrifying and huge God inside of us. When you believe that and act like it, you will be shocked at what you start seeing.

It is not enough to be passionate. The thought that I could be passionately wrong about who the Father is and what He expects scares me half to death. If we judge ourselves and others on the basis of our passion alone, then what makes us different from the men who flew the planes into the Twin Towers? They were serving their god passionately.

We must be willing to let His presence define normal, fearless Christianity in our lives. Our Father does not want to be studied like a subject in school. He wants to be engaged and then released to a broken world.

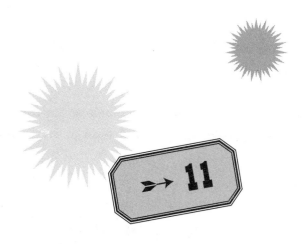

# When Healing Does Not Come

I have had the opportunity to watch the impossibly good happen in people's lives. I have also witnessed the darkness of pain and tragedy. I have prayed with expectation that people would be released in this life into fields of peace and joy only to see them pass on to the afterlife.

How do we deal with these opposite outcomes of prayer—life and death? How do we accept heaven's invitation to do the Father's works if defeat is a brutal reality?

Praying for people who either got sicker or died has caused me to ask the toughest questions of my life. Those of us who have prayed heaven down on someone and watched that person die understand how difficult this is. To me, all of the Father's beloved children are heroes, but the heroes who stand out above the rest are those who have experienced the worst life could throw at them and still choose to believe in the Father's goodness and desire to set captives free.

I have met two of these heroes, a couple at our church. Their names are Richard and Cristi. I want to share their story, told from Cristi's perspective in a journal entry.

*March 8, 2011*

*It wasn't until last year that I asked the Father why Hannah died. It's not that I was afraid to, or that I was angry. I wasn't. I always knew that He was good, and that there was a bigger picture. I simply didn't feel the need to know. I had always believed for a miracle. I lived every day as her mom filled with hope. There were many, many painful days, but never any hopeless ones. She was a beautiful and perfect gift to us and I rejoiced over her every day of her life. She made me better. I didn't expect to lose her, but on March 8, 1995, Richard woke me in the very early morning to tell me that the life was gone from her precious little body. I was shocked. I was numb. I learned what it was to grieve, and to be comforted. Family and friends were there for us. Richard was amazing; a rock of strength and a soft place to land at the same time. And my Father never left me. He was faithful as always.*

*Last year, fifteen years later, I asked the Father why. The answer was simple and yet profound. Hannah was a very blessed little girl. She was the most joyful and content child I've ever known. Her physical and mental abilities were severely limited, but her spirit soared.*

*She had a direct line to heaven. Her fellowship with the Father was unhindered. So, while I prayed for a miracle, she simply desired more and more of Him. She had already tasted heaven. And when both of our requests were heard—hers trumped mine. How could I argue with that?*

*My heart is at rest. I did experience disappointment for many years over not getting my miracle. I will always miss her sweet presence in our lives. Grief still visits my heart at unexpected times, catching me by surprise and bringing me to tears. But with each year that passes I become more and more convinced of His love and His goodness. I still believe in miracles and fully expect to see them. I know that my heavenly Father was not the author of my precious Hannah's suffering, but as one of my favorite authors says, "God is so big that He can win with any hand." As circumstances go, we were dealt a bad hand, but in Hannah's short life and in her death, we most definitely won! I love the way the Bible says it:*

In all these things we are more than conquerors through him who loved us. For I am convinced that neither death nor life, neither angels nor demons, neither the present nor the future, nor any powers, neither height nor depth, nor anything else in all creation, will be able to separate us from the love of God that is in Christ Jesus our Lord.

Romans 8:37–40

*He is really, really good! Can you taste it? Hannah did. She now has a continual feast. And one day we will feast together.*

## Healing vs. Disappointment

As I minister to people, I encounter many different thoughts on tragedy and the role the Father plays in it. Some people say that God dealt a mighty blow. Other people say that mysteries are simply mysteries, and we will never fully understand.

I wrestle with this. The Father has shown me what my future holds—that I will continue to experience the naturally supernatural the rest of my life. As much as I am excited about that, I also seem to be drawn to people who never experience breakthrough. I think it is because of the death of my Papa and the pain that came with it. I have compassion for other people who do not have a lot of reason to believe in the goodness of a kind God.

I love when people receive dramatic breakthrough for their needs, but I also feel deep sympathy when their longing for wholeness is unfulfilled. For whatever reason, I am not obsessed with the whys and why nots. In order to develop a lifestyle of being naturally supernatural, we have to get to the place where we no longer need to explain why something did or did not happen.

I read the story of a man of faith and how he struggles with this as well. He has seen miracles all over the world while watching his own mother die of sickness. He knows of nothing else to do but to continue praying for the sick.

As disciples, that is what we are commanded to do. If that makes you cringe, I understand. I cannot tell you how many times I have told the Lord that His commands frustrate me. Reading the gospels and wrestling with them has not always brought peace, but it has given me direction.

I follow that direction even when it leads to seasons of great struggle.

When I am around people like Richard and Cristi, I am overwhelmed with emotion. They have confronted death and survived. And instead of growing bitter and walking away from the supernatural, they have chosen a church fellowship where the supernatural has become valued and expected.

Why do some run from the supernatural and others run toward it? I do not know, though I have observed that people who run from the Father's works are often living in places of deep disappointment and pain—personal hells of failed expectations. Maybe the world is waiting for people who demonstrate that it is possible to walk through the choppy waters of unanswered prayer with peaceful assurance that God is still good.

One afternoon a few years ago, I had the opportunity to pray for a beautiful teenage girl who lived in my hometown. She was battling cancer. Her dad had had a tremendous impact on my life when I was a young man, and I was really excited about praying for her. The week before, I had seen two or three people receive healing from the Father, and I was 100 percent sure that we would see a miracle in her case as well. As I prayed for her, I was overwhelmed by her maturity and love for Jesus Christ. She truly was remarkable.

Instead of recovering from cancer, a few days later she went to be with the Father. When I got the news, I went to the lowest place in my journey of signs and wonders. I told the Lord exactly what I thought about the fact that this young girl had died. I withdrew from praying for anyone. I screamed at heaven: "No wonder so many people won't touch this stuff with a ten-foot pole!" I was furious. I remember thinking,

*Why in the world would I want to go after the Kingdom when defeat is such a common reality?*

The human heart is a mysterious thing and, at that point, my heart was far away from pursuing Him and His Kingdom. Thank God He is big enough to hear all of our complaints. He was gentle with me as I wrestled with what keeps most disciples from believing for great things.

After a few weeks, I felt Him wooing me back to a place of friendship and intimacy. Then something happened that I believe will define me for the rest of my life. In the wake of this young girl's death, I told the Lord, "I will do what You have commanded Your disciples to do even if it never makes sense to me. I will simply love." Something started changing inside of me and is continuing to change even now in my pursuit of Jesus.

This whole Kingdom story is about love. Have you ever noticed how many times the Bible says, "Jesus was moved with compassion and . . ."? It is not about the healings or miracles in themselves. Healings come and go. Miracles are here and gone. Love remains. Even when I am praying for someone and nothing is manifesting I can love with compassion and grace. I can choose to focus on the most important thing: love.

Read 1 John 4:8: "God is love." It is all about love. I have had a sinus infection this past week while writing about being naturally supernatural. I have prayed over it, my friends have prayed over it and it is not getting better. But I am not going to condemn myself. I am going to focus on His love for me and move forward.

It is not unusual to see people struggle with physical issues while praying for someone else who is healed. A few weeks ago, I was standing on a stage in Haiti preaching on these things. I cannot think of a time in my life when I was sicker than I was during that sermon. I had eaten some slaw at the Port au Prince airport, which is about as wise as sipping Lysol. I felt as though I had a fever of two hundred degrees. I had practically rubbed the hair off of my head I prayed over myself so much. Nothing happened. I would not have minded if Abba had just taken me to glory. But that night, I prayed for someone and saw him dramatically touched by the Father.

What do you do with that? What do you do when you have the flu, and you pray for someone else with the flu, and that person is healed immediately, but you are still sick? What I do is keep moving forward in love. We love ourselves in the middle of our own messes, and we love others when their dreams of wholeness are not fulfilled.

In the past couple of years I have seen God bring breakthrough as I have prayed for people, while one of my best friends has gone through his own personal battle with the sickness of his son. The things this family has experienced—multiple surgeries, hundreds of hours of tears, disappointments and failed expectations—have kept me up late on many nights. It is not an easy thing to wrestle with.

But I am called to do the Father's works, and His kindness is what gets me back on track. Without His ridiculous love and gentleness, I do not know what I would do. I daydream sometimes about how awesome it will be in heaven with no sickness to pray for. In the meantime I think it is possible to experience breakthrough while also embracing the tension that comes when expectations are not met. Living a life with no offense toward God or anyone else when things are not going our way brings freedom that I pray I can embrace.

## Healing and Doctors

Personally, I love doctors. I have two good friends who are doctors. When I am not feeling good and prayer seems to be doing nothing, I go see my doctors and ask for help. Whether I am getting the Father's love through a doctor or directly from heaven through prayer is fine with me.

The point is, Jesus is a healer, not a hurter. A new message of gentleness, grace and compassion is emerging when it comes to the supernatural. Look at the Master, Teacher, Big Brother, High Priest and Savior. How did He operate in the works of the Father? He seemed to be gentle and unassuming—never making a spectacle of Himself. The only time He got really riled up was toward the religious community.

It is fine to dissect the pros and cons of the supernatural, but I want to be among those who are engaged in conversation while demonstrating the Kingdom. If those around us who have doubts and fears can see normal, everyday people demonstrating the Father's works, I think they will be quicker to act like biblical disciples themselves.

I was in Chicago recently at a conference for thousands of people going after the Kingdom. During one of the breaks between sessions, I felt led to go to one of the large stores in the area. When I arrived, the Father told me to go talk with a group of students shopping there.

One of the young men was named George. He was a neat guy with a neat story. He is Haitian, and he has been asking the Father to send him to a ministry in Haiti that focuses on intercession. His mouth dropped when I told him what we are doing in Haiti. George went to Haiti with us, and he will never be the same person as a result of what the Father did in his life. Only a Father of love and compassion would orchestrate something like that.

## The Ultimate Destination

When I was a child, I loved to play in a field near our house. There were huge power lines near that field, and I thought they were the coolest things. I would lie on the ground and look up at those lines, daydreaming that they were part of a spaceship power plant.

One afternoon in that field, I was a little more contemplative than usual. I can still see that sky in my mind as I spotted "animals" in the cloud formations. Then, for the first time in my life, I thought about heaven.

It was around the time Papa died, and I am sure that is what got me thinking about heaven. I had heard so many adults talking about Papa being in heaven that it was natural to think about it. Even as a five-year-old, I found peace thinking about heaven. I imagined who was there, what it looked like and what in the world people did in that place.

In recent years, I have found myself daydreaming about heaven again. I will probably not go back to that field and stare at the power lines, but the older I get, the more childlike I am trying to become. Children love using their imaginations, so I try to use my imagination to ponder what it would look like if heaven had an impact on the world in which I live right now. Many times I have told the Lord how jealous I am of the early disciples who got to see heaven explode in this realm while He was here.

Let's welcome that realm here and now. Let's choose to press on. The next time someone has a headache near you, I invite you to say, "This is going to sound strange to you, but would you mind if I lay my hands on your head and pray that you feel better?"

We will never have all the answers, but at some point we all have to decide whether or not to obey Jesus' command—regardless of how it turns out.

At this point in my life I am starting to realize that as long as I live on this planet, I will have trouble. Jesus warned us of this (see John 16:33). When pain, disappointment and tragedy rear their ugly heads, we are left trying to make sense of it, and the only sense we *can* make of it is to believe in the goodness of God no matter what.

When tragedy wins the battle, we do not declare that God is getting glory from our lack of breakthrough. No, we embrace the messiness of following a Savior in an unseen realm while our lives on earth have blood on the trail.

At some point this whole thing will come to an end and I am sure all of us will have a lot of questions. Until then, we have the opportunity to move past our fears and attempt to live the life that is presented in the gospels through the person of Jesus.

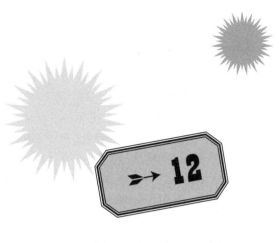

# Go for It

Every man deserves to own a nice riding lawnmower at some point in his life. A John Deere tractor can make a man feel important. Grabbing a twelve-ounce can of cold Coca-Cola and cranking up your own lawnmower beast can serve as the highlight of the week.

One beautiful fall afternoon some years ago, my yard provided the perfect atmosphere for just such a highlight. I am a grass man. I am not talking about the illegal stuff. I am talking about fescue, Bermuda, zoysia and centipede. I love the look of a well-manicured lawn. On this particular day, my fescue was thick and begging for a trim. I popped in a sermon on my iPod, took my shirt off, cranked up the tractor, and began to listen to a man talk about how to hear the voice of God. I do not remember who he was, but I do remember saying out loud, "God, I want to start hearing You speak to me more. I want to start hearing You more."

As I was about to finish cutting the grass, my wife walked outside and said, "Why do you not have a shirt on and do you know where Sam's pacifier is?" If you are a parent, you know that losing a pacifier is worse than losing thousands of dollars in the stock market. Pacifiers keep the world peaceful. The first thought that came to mind was, *Ask God*. At that point, I was just getting to know Him as Father and to relate to Him in more intimate ways.

So I prayed this prayer: "Father, where is Sam's pacifier?" Immediately I heard in my mind, *Between the mattress and springs*. I told Wendy that God said it was in his crib.

She stared at me and said, "Chad, I am not in the mood for one of your jokes." I remember thinking that undoubtedly I was crazy, and that I needed to be careful because this was a strange spiritual rabbit trail.

But ten minutes later, Wendy came outside and said, "I went to look for the pacifier where you said it was and didn't see it. After a few minutes, I went back up there again and it was exactly where you said it was." I cannot describe exactly what I felt, but I knew in my spirit that I was about to start hearing His voice more and more.

The reason that many of us never hear His voice is that we do not think we can. It is amazing what happens when we act in faith and try to hear Him. A young lady went to Haiti with our group. At the beginning of the trip, she was hesitant to pray for anyone on our own team, much less people she had never met. But after a few days, she was praying for the sick and getting prophetic words for others. There need to be a lot more people like her in the world. I hope that our Father will use this book to turn you into one of them.

The King often said, "Let it be done to you as you have believed" or "Your faith has made you whole." If you believe you can hear Him and are willing to be patient and be trained, you will be amazed at what He can do through you. On the other hand, if you believe you *cannot* hear Him, you *will not* hear Him. Faith comes from great love, and when you are walking in intimacy with Him, your faith will go through the roof. When others roll their eyes and judge you for attempting to know Him in this way, just smile and say, "Abba, You are worth it."

## A New World

Take a look around. The game is changing. The voices quick to label things of the Holy Spirit as "strange" are rapidly being drowned out by normal, messy people who are walking in the works of the Father. No longer does a "faith healer" come to town to see a bunch of works manifest. No, these are the days when a seventh-grade girl prays for one of her friends at school and sees her healed right there in her lunchroom. We are rapidly moving into the world of college students putting down their arguments for a while and actually praying for people the way that Stephen, Philip, Andrew, Peter and James did. Who knows? Perhaps we are in the days where normal, messy people are getting the courage to pray for the dead to be raised.

I want to be part of this move of the Father. I love Jesus with all of my heart, and the message I see sweeping the world is His message of the love of the Father and the arrival of His works through us.

At our church, we have seen many people renewed in their understanding of who they are in Christ. Now we are seeing that understanding expand itself into doing the Father's works—not just the superstars of faith but also normal people like you and me. This is what Jesus was most concerned about while He was here, and it is what He is turning the Church back toward.

## Team Time

On our mission trips, we enjoy devoting time to praying for each team member. I have been a part of many of these prayer times and have seen some wonderful breakthroughs. One person who stands out in my mind is April Boyer. On a mission trip to Haiti, April experienced the healing that Jesus offers. I want you to hear her story in her own words.

The events most significant in your life are ones that split your timeline into *before* and *after*. You will need to understand my *before* so you can grasp the impact of my *after*.

Discovering I was pregnant thrilled my husband and me. I worked full time, so, understandably, my first trimester exhausted me. I colonized the couch each evening, my husband catering to all my needs. Weeks passed, and in my second trimester my energy improved. Still I remained on the couch. I cried over the smallest things. My motivation to do anything simply faded.

Physically, pregnancy was kind to me. What little morning sickness I experienced departed after the first three months. I had none of the typical pregnancy woes: heartburn, backaches or swelling. And yet . . . a fog had settled. It was heavy, dense and it wouldn't leave. *It will get better* became my mantra, and I convinced myself that if these emotional afflictions were my biggest hurdle, then surely I could manage. The tipping point for getting help came during a trip home for the holidays. I sat in a room full of laughing friends and felt utterly and hopelessly alone.

I called my doctor. Medicine was prescribed. I sobbed in my husband's arms after picking up my prescription. The prescription warnings for pregnant women were horrifying. Feeling trapped and fearful, we prayed over the pills. "Father, please protect my baby. I don't know what else to do." The pills lightened the load, and I was more functional, but the damage was done. A fault line had developed in my psyche. I still wasn't quite "me."

My daughter arrived on this earth, incredibly tiny and completely perfect. I wanted nothing more than to be her everything. The level of functionality I had achieved the few months before her birth remained consistent during her first year. The leaching had ceased, but the rest of me was still MIA. I went through the motions and was confident I was meeting her needs, but numbness stood between the connection of head and heart. I knew in my mind how much I loved my daughter. I looked at her and was consciously aware of how much she meant to me, but I couldn't access the emotions. They were corked like champagne, struggling to get out.

The thought of having more children petrified me. My recurring thought was, *If I have another baby, that'll be the end of me. I'll never come back from that.* I just knew that another pregnancy would cause the fault line to fracture. I held out for rescue, knowing deep in my soul that this could not possibly be the future to which I was relegated.

My Haiti trip was almost a year in the making. When my family and I first attended what would later become our church home, a team had just been sent out. An announcement was made concerning future trips, and something inside me stirred. I knew I was supposed to go. I questioned what I could possibly offer, but still, the sensation persisted.

For the next several months, all my plans focused on going to Haiti. The weeks leading up to the trip I downplayed its significance, unsure of its purpose and, quite honestly, fearful of expecting too much.

We arrived on a Friday. On Saturday morning we sat together for "team time"; I was a mix of emotions. As two other teammates told their stories, I watched out of the window as two little Haitian boys played next to the tent in which they lived. I longed for compassion for them, could muster very little and returned to the thought, *What's wrong with me?*

Then it was someone else's turn for team time. Chad asked out loud, "Father, who is next?"

I caught Chad's eye and he immediately called me forward, smiling that "I know our Father is up to something" kind of smile.

I began by giving my church background, how I grew up, how I got to be on this Haiti trip. A few people offered encouraging words, and then Chad asked the question, "Do you want more children?"

I could barely eke out the sound: "Maybe."

Chad asked me, "What's going on there?" And with that simple question, the pain of the past two years came bubbling out. Chad and some other team members got up and began to pray for me. With his hand on my head, mine on my stomach, he began to talk to the Lord. He asked the team for confirmation: "What is the endocrine system?" They responded that it has to do with hormones. Chad, listening to the Lord, said, "This is just hormones." He commanded them to realign. He spoke wholeness over my body and my mind.

His words continued, but I no longer heard them. I was sobbing into my free hand, completely broken before the Lord. I needed whatever He was offering me. I had nothing else to give.

Warmth spread across my abdomen. An exchange was made. The fog, the darkness, all the heaviness from the past two years began to recede. I could feel the Father drawing it out of me as one draws poison from a wound. I was cognizant only of the Lord's presence enveloping my body and mind. I imagined the room to be thick with it. We stayed that way for an indeterminate amount of time. Eventually the world came back into view. I knew something was different. I had just experienced a miracle.

I spent the rest of our week praying for people, dancing with Haitian children, and trying to figure out what that new feeling of lightness would look like when I got back to my regular life. When we started to head home, the emotions were mixed. I dreaded leaving, but longed to tell my husband, "You have your wife back." I thought of my daughter, my sweet baby girl, and how the love I have for her would finally be able to flow freely, no longer hampered or disabled.

As I write this story down, it is just shy of a year since that trip to Haiti. These several months have been nothing short of wild. The Father did not just restore me in Haiti; He changed me. I returned with energy coursing through my veins, feeling more alive than at any other point in my life. Everything is possible now—both a frightening and exhilarating proposition, the very definition of what my church family calls "wrecked." The best of what my future holds is yet to be seen.

As I share this story, I am six weeks pregnant with our second child. And I want you to know this baby was planned. The Father did not blindside me with some happy surprise. We are walking into this with eyes wide open, brimming with an inner assurance that it simply will be different this time. I could drive myself crazy with a barrage of "Why me's?" and visit that place of fear where the "What if's?" creep in, but I am resolved never to give those thoughts a foothold in my life. All those questions are part of my *before*, and I, praise God, I am living in my *after*.

The Father was in Jesus and Jesus is in us (see John 17:23). Jesus told His disciples: "As the Father has loved me, so have I loved you. Now remain in my love" (John 15:9). Our goal should be to have the courage to release the love of the Father and Son in whatever situations we find ourselves. The next time you are around someone with a great need, say to him or her, "The God of the universe is my Father. He lives inside of me. Can I pray for you and release His love and power to you?" Be willing to be available when the Kingdom comes calling.

## Splashdown

Last spring I was playing in a golf tournament with my best buddies. We are like kids at this tournament every year. It is our chance to compete against each other as though the world depended on it. We take this tournament so seriously that you would probably think we are ridiculous.

Late one afternoon, we were playing in a format that always produces a little drama. It is a sixteen-man match, with four teams of four competing. With two holes to play, we knew that our four-man group had a great chance to win the match. We could hear the yells coming from other groups elsewhere on the course, and so we knew that we had to finish strong.

I was the last member of our foursome to hit a shot on hole 16. It was 110 yards to the hole. When I made contact with the ball, I said out loud, "Get in the hole." The ball landed on the green, rolled five feet, and disappeared into the cup.

I was so overcome with excitement that I did not know what to do other than start running. The three guys in my group came running after me to tackle me for a wild celebration together. Instead of letting them catch me, I made a beeline for the nastiest-looking pond in North America. It is the kind of pond that frogs stay out of so as not to get a disease.

Have you ever had a moment that felt like slow motion? This was one for me. When my feet left solid earth and I curled into the cannonball position, I thought, *What am I doing?* Moments later I hit that nasty, chilly water and sank to the bottom like a slab of bricks. I have never gotten out of a body of water so fast in my life. Yet as I was climbing out—seeing all my buddies doubled over with laughter—I soaked it all in because I felt totally alive. Making an eagle on a par 4 was fun, but what made it even better was sprinting to that pond like a wild man. Playing the last two holes drenched was funny as well.

There were ten reasons I should not have done a cannonball into that pond, including the fact that I coughed up green stuff for three days; lost a pair of $200 Maui Jim sunglasses that were a gift; ruined my golf shoes, belt, shorts and shirt; lost my hat; and almost broke my ankle when I slammed into whatever was at the bottom of the pond. But none of that really mattered. What mattered was that I made a memory that I will have for the rest of my life.

At the end of our lives, I have a feeling we will wish we had taken a few more risks. When a minister who was a mentor of mine retired, he told my dad that he wished he had taken more risks in ministry. One of my biggest fears in life is realizing at the end of it that I played it too safe. So I am going for it. Sometimes walking in the Father's works will get you persecuted, judged and misunderstood. The disappointment that comes when you do not see someone experience healing can bring you to your knees.

Yet in the middle of all of that, there is a little whisper from the King: "Whoever believes in me will do the works I have been doing, and they will do even greater things than these, because I am going to the Father" (John 14:12).

The Father is worth it. Jesus is worth it. The Holy Spirit is worth it. You will never know unless you go for it. I hope that this book has encouraged you to jump in with both feet.

Early in my journey, I was talking to a good friend about the Father. We were discussing passionately what it will be like one day finally to meet the God of the universe. I said, "I can't wait to leap into His lap." I yearn for the day in which I can run right past everyone in glory land and go straight to Him. I have told Jesus many times, "I love You, but take me right to the Father." I am sure He smiles.

Watching the Father's love flow through my hands and help someone in dramatic ways is always thrilling. Realizing He actually likes me never gets old. When you believe that you matter to Him and that He has a picture of you in His wallet, the world settles down a little bit.

So my plan is simply to help others discover what I have discovered. It is not about signs and wonders. It is not about prophetic words. It is not about encounters with angels or open visions. It is about growing in deep friendship with the Father, Jesus and the Holy Spirit.

The other night I went to a Coldplay concert with my wife. The song "Paradise" was blaring, and as I sang at the top of my lungs I began to let the tears flow from my eyes. After a few seconds, a dam seemed to burst in my belly. As I listened to the words it all started to hit home with me. The girl in the song goes through the hardship of life yet still believes in a greater existence than what she is experiencing.

It would be great if life were one big vacation. It would be incredible if there were no such thing as conflict, confusion, doubt or pain. Yet all of us are aware of the realities of living in this world. I have yet to meet anyone who does not know what it is like to hurt.

In the middle of all of our stories we are left to imagine and believe in a reality that is greater than any story ever dreamed up by Hollywood. If we choose, our reality can mean not only that a King and His Father await us on the other side, but also that they are eager to influence this world now with their love and power.

As we trek through this messy life, we have the promise of the Holy Spirit never to leave or forsake us as we attempt to bring that Kingdom here. In the wins and losses, we celebrate knowing that one day all will be well. In the meantime, we get to choose whether or not we will go for it. We get to make a decision not just to read about Jesus but actually to live as He lived while He was here. I made up my mind ten years ago to do that. There is no going back.

If you would like to join me on this journey, here is a prayer to be naturally supernatural.

*Father,*

*As I read Your Word and watch Your Son move throughout the pages of the Scriptures, I notice that He helped many people in unusual ways. I am asking You, Father, to help me ease into this reality for my own life. Would You please teach me how to be more naturally supernatural? Please open my eyes to who I am in Jesus, and how I can make John 14:12 a reality in my own life. I confess to You, Father, that I don't know everything. I humble myself before Your feet and ask that You use me to set people free—just like my heroes that I read about in the New Testament. Please show me how I can believe You for great things. My hands are Yours. My heart is Yours. Teach me not only how to learn what Jesus taught, but also how to operate in Your works as He did. Give me a sense of awareness of how clean I am in Your eyes. My life is Yours. I want to emulate my King. I want to know You the way in which Jesus knew You while He operated on the earth. I want to grow in intimacy with the Holy Spirit. Show Your power through my weakness. In the name of Jesus Christ I pray. Amen.*

## Appendix

# Truths of the Father

As I have come to know the Father better, one of the things that helps me grow in intimacy with Him is repeating truths about Him aloud. This is by no means a complete list, but I wanted to share it in the hope that it might help you as much as it has helped me. I have found that faith rises up in me as I speak these things out loud. When I first started doing this I thought, *This is crazy.* Ten years later, I am convinced it is not crazy. You have to start somewhere. If you learn to think as He thinks, you will see what He sees.

Father is giving.

Father is compassionate.

Father is loving.

Father is kind.

Father is gentle.

Father is forgiving.

Father is inviting.

Father is encouraging.

Father is tender.

Father is caring.

Father is healer.

Father is pleased.

Father is relentless.

Father is happy.

Father is abundant.

Father is joyful.

Father is complete.

Father is stress-free.v

Father is warm.

Father is friendly.

Father is appealing.

Father is fun.

Father is empathizing.

Father is present.

Father is real.

Father is gracious.

Father is graceful.

Father is light.

➤—→

**Chad Norris** is Pastor of Life Transformation at City Church in Simpsonville, South Carolina. Since joining the church staff in 2010, he has served as a teacher, discipler and mission team leader to Haiti. Before joining the City Church staff, he co-founded Wayfarer. With that ministry he served as a writer and speaker—publishing seven different Bible study titles and traveling to speak to students, children and adults at churches, camps, retreats and other events throughout the country. He has also served as college minister at the Church of Brook Hills in Birmingham, Alabama. Chad is a graduate of the University of Georgia and of Beeson Divinity School. Chad and his wife, Wendy, have three children, Sam, Ruthie and Jack.

You may reach Chad at chad@wearecitychurch.com.

For further information, please visit www.chadnorris.com or find him on Facebook at Facebook.com/author.chadnorris.

To book Chad to speak at your event,
visit *chadnorris.com*
or *facebook.com / author.chadnorris*
or contact him at
*chad@wearecitychurch.com.*